CIRCLES OF LEARNING

Cooperation in the Classroom

David W. Johnson
Roger T. Johnson
Edythe Johnson Holubec
Patricia Roy

About the Authors

David W. Johnson is Professor of Educational Psychology, and Roger T. Johnson is Professor of Curriculum and Instruction; both are Co-Directors of the Cooperative Learning Center, University of Minnesota, Minneapolis. Their sister, Edythe Johnson Holubec, is Instructor, English Department, the University of Texas at Austin. Patricia Roy is Coordinator, Effective Schools Center, Educational Cooperative Service Unit of the Twin Cities Metropolitan Area, Minneapolis.

Printed in the United States of America

Printing by Edwards Brothers, Inc., 1984, 1988
Composition by Scott Photographics, Inc.

Price: $8.50
ASCD Stock Number: 611-84324
ISBN: 0-87120-123-2
Library of Congress Card Catalog Number: 83-083395

Contents

DEDICATION

This book is dedicated to our parents,
Roger and Frances Johnson
and
Gerald and Stefanie Rose,
who discouraged inappropriate competition
and taught us to cooperate

ACKNOWLEDGMENTS

Thanks are due to the thousands of teachers who have taken their training in structuring cooperative learning groups back into the classroom and created an environment where students care about each other and each other's learning. They have taught us a lot over the years.

A special thanks to Judy Bartlett, our office manager at the Cooperative Learning Center, who deals with people with charm and patience, and an even more difficult task, deals with us with charm and patience. She went far beyond the call of duty (as she always does) to get this book in print.

ACKNOWLEDGMENTS

Foreword

It is very common for critics in education to view learning as individualistic and competitive acts. Schools seldom provide for cooperative planning for teachers. Teachers, in turn, rarely provide for cooperative practices to take place in the classroom.

We are entering an educational era that will change all that. Improving instruction and providing more effective learning will be easier to implement effectively if it focuses on "we" classrooms, coupled with the theme of "we are all involved in this together."

Today, cooperative learning processes have been rediscovered and are being used throughout the country on every level.

This book has several key messages that are invaluable for all educators. The dominant aim in the classroom should be cooperation. The basic elements of the cooperative aim structure are positive interdependence, individual accountability, face-to-face interaction, and cooperative skills. Students should always be made aware that their performance will be to "sink or swim together" in a cooperative learning setting. Teachers must be prepared to teach needed collaborative skills in order for cooperative learning to be productive. The success of implementing cooperative learning in the classroom rests on professional support from principals, teachers, and other staff members—but most of all, on cooperating with each other.

LAWRENCE S. FINKEL
President, 1983-84
Association for Supervision and
Curriculum Development

Why Cooperative Learning Is Important

In every classroom, teachers may structure lessons so that students are in a win-lose struggle to see who is best. They can also allow students to learn on their own, individually, or they can arrange students in pairs or small groups to help each other master the assigned material.

An essential instructional skill that all teachers need is knowing how and when to structure students' learning goals competitively, individualistically, and cooperatively. Each goal structure has its place; an effective teacher will use all three appropriately.

The Choice

Teachers can structure lessons *competitively* so that students work against each other to achieve a goal that only one or a few students can attain. Students are graded on a curve, which requires them to work faster and more accurately than their peers. In such competitive situations there is a negative interdependence among goal achievements; students perceive that they can obtain their goals if and only if the other students in the class fail to obtain their goals (Deutsch, 1962; Johnson and Johnson, 1975). Thus, a student seeks an outcome that is personally beneficial but is detrimental to the others with whom he or she is competitively linked. Unfortunately, most students perceive school as predominantly a competitive enterprise. They either constantly work hard in school to do better than the other students, or they take it easy because they do not believe they have a chance to win.

Teachers can structure lessons *individualistically* so that students work by themselves to accomplish learning goals unrelated to those of the other students. Individual goals are assigned each day, students' efforts are evaluated on a fixed set of standards, and rewards are given accordingly. Each student has a set of materials and works at his or her own speed, ignoring the progress of other students in the class. In individualistic learning situations, students' goal achievements are independent; students perceive that the achievement of their learning goals is unrelated to what other students do (Deutsch, 1962; Johnson and Johnson, 1975). Whether a student accomplishes his or her goal has no influence on whether other students achieve their goals in an individualistic learning situation. Thus, a student seeks an outcome that is personally beneficial and ignores as irrelevant the goal achievement of other students.

For the past half century competitive and individualistic goal structures have dominated American education. Students usually come to school with competitive expectations and pressures from their parents. Many teachers have tried to reduce classroom competition by switching from a norm-referenced to a criteria-referenced evaluation system. In both competitive and individualistic learning situations, teachers try to keep students away from each other.

There is a third option. Teachers can structure lessons *cooperatively* so that students work together to accomplish shared goals. Students are assigned to small groups and instructed to learn the assigned material and to make sure that the other members of the group learn the assigned material. Individual accountability can be checked randomly by selecting a paper from each group to grade. A criteria-referenced evaluation system is used.

In cooperative learning situations, there is a positive interdependence among students' goal attainments; students perceive that they can reach their learning goals if and only if the other students in the learning group also reach their goals (Deutsch, 1962; Johnson and Johnson, 1975). Thus, students seek outcomes that are beneficial to all those with whom they are cooperatively linked. Students discuss the material with each other, help one another understand it, and encourage each other to work hard. Yet if cooperative relationships are the *only* way students interact in school, they may never learn to compete appropriately for fun or have the opportunity to follow a learning trail on their own.

Crisis in Achievement

An achievement crisis exists in our schools and is reflected in the following trends, confirmed by research:

1. *SAT Scores.* Although more students are staying in school longer and going on to college, all signs indicate that they are less well-equipped in basic skills than their predecessors. The average scores on the College Entrance Examination Board's Scholastic Aptitude Test, for example, have declined steadily during the past 20 years (Johnson and Johnson, 1983, and others). Only in 1982 was there a leveling off and even a miniscule upturn. The number of high achievers (those scoring over 600) on the SAT has been dropping, and the scores of top students (valedictorians and salutatorians) show a similar decline.

2. *Quality of Work Force.* The quality of the work force is defined as acquired abilities of the population—their education, experience, skills, health, creativity, motivation, and entrepreneurism (Becker, 1975). Traditionally, in the United States, half of our growth in productivity comes from increases in individuals' skills and knowledge. But such growth in the U.S. has fallen off. Our productive growth now is below that of major European nations, not to mention that of Japan. If we do not invest more in people—and soon—we will get precious little out of our machines; the economic health and future of America is at stake. (Becker, 1975; Schultz, 1981).

3. *Science and Math Education.* For the past 15 years or so, the science and math achievement of our students has been falling relative to the other industrialized countries in the world. Science is not well liked by teachers and students in the United States. Nor is it stressed by schools. Elementary school students are lucky if they receive 20 minutes of science a day; 50 percent of the high school students in the U.S. take no science courses after grade 10. Moreover, many high schools now lack qualified math or science teachers on their staffs—the competition from industry is too strong for trained people to bother with teaching. Despite the lure of ready, high-salaried jobs, the percentage of seniors intending to major in all sciences and related subjects, such as engineering in college, declined from 39 percent in 1965 to 19 percent in 1975 and will decline to a projected 15 percent in 1985, if present trends continue (R. Johnson and Johnson, 1982c; Science Education Data book, 1980; Walberg, 1982).

   Only 500,000 U.S. students take calculus in high school or college, while in the Soviet Union, according to Wirszup (1981), 5 million secondary school students complete a one-year course in calculus. All youth, the Soviets claim, are required to complete five years of physics, four of chemistry, and up to four years of biology by the end of secondary school (which nearly all students complete). The math-science achievements of our students trail behind students of top-ranking little New Zealand, the United Kingdom, Hungary, Sweden, and Finland. (Comber and Reeves, 1973). Clearly, deemphasizing science and math education limits our economic, defense, and social capacities.

4. *Functional Illiteracy.* There is a saying, "If you think education is expensive, try ignorance!" This comment is not so funny in the light of the functional illiteracy that seems to be increasing both among those students who drop out of school and even those who finish high school. In 1975, about 20 percent of all American 17-year-olds were functionally illiterate; they failed to respond correctly to simple written questions about everyday life in our modern society—how to read directions on a package, for example, or how to balance a checkbook (Lerner, 1981). According to the 1976 National Assessment of Educational Progress (NAEP), fewer 17-year-olds (53.9 percent as opposed to 64.4 in 1969) knew simple details about how our government functions.

A Crisis in Socialization

A substantial number of children, teenagers, and young adults feel isolated, disconnected from their parents and peers, unattached to school and career, without purpose and direction, and lacking any distinct impression of who and what kind of persons they are (D. Johnson, 1979, 1980b). Many are out of touch with the rest of society, unable to build and maintain real connections with others. Not only is this a cruel waste for the young people afflicted, it means they can begin to exploit or abuse others without guilt or remorse, people who have no motivation to contribute to the well-being of others or of society. The evidence is shown in the following:

1. The dramatic increase through the 1960s and 1970s of the frequency with which juveniles are involved in serious crimes against property (such as burglary, auto theft, larceny, arson, and vandalism). Enough of this criminal activity takes place within schools to make it a serious drain on educational resources that should be more productively used. The annual cost to repair the damage done to school

property, for example, is more than $200 million. There is the time lost and the human damage, as well; 2.4 million students and 128,000 teachers report having something stolen in a typical month, and 282,000 students and 5,200 teachers report being physically assaulted in a typical month (Bybee and Gee, 1982).

2. The rise of more than 250 percent in the suicide rate among teenagers and 150 percent among children 5 to 14 years of age over the past 20 years (Bronfenbrenner, 1976). One out of every 640 high school students will commit suicide this year; ten will make a serious attempt to kill themselves; and 100 will contemplate doing so.

3. The presence of a permanent criminal underclass that is totally out of touch with the rest of society. Auletta, in his book *The Underclass*, states, "I have met 15-year-olds who will kill absolutely without remorse. They are especially antagonized by any of the usual symbols of authority, property, office, and so on." What is new today, writes Silberman in *Criminal Violence, Criminal Justice*, is that people will "kill, maim, and injure without reason or remorse." Random and senseless murders committed by people who do not know their victims have been increasing twice as fast as other murders since the 1960s. The presence of a permanent criminal underclass presents a severe drain on our society.

4. A general social malaise characterized by a loss of confidence in our future and in our ability to solve our societal problems. Twelve Americanists (all dons at Oxford University, England) recently completed a study entitled, *America in Perspective: Major Trends in the United States Through the 1980s*. One of the major themes the book identified as running through our cultural, economic, and political life is a general social malaise resulting in large numbers of people who are demoralized and who view attempts to solve our national and world problems as hopeless and beyond our capabilities.

5. Changes in the family through divorce affect twice as many students as were affected 20 years ago. Moreover, one of every five families in the U.S. is now supported by a woman. Although more than half our work force is female, women still earn less than men, on most jobs. Latch-key children are commonplace now, nor are they necessarily children of the poor. Many middle-class wives work to augment their husbands' incomes in order to provide their children with the college education they consider so important—and to keep up a life-style that is increasingly costly. As a result, children spend less time with their parents, more time with their peers, or are simply on their own in a confusing world. And these are the kids who are

"well-off." Children in poor, single-family households are that much more beleaguered.

The roots of student alienation lie in the stress and the lack of caring and support in their families, their educational and community experiences. Family disorganization, particularly, has been shown to be an antecedent to behavior disorders, lack of school achievement, and pathology in children and adolescents (Bronfenbrenner, 1976).

What Can We Do?

Unfortunately, some of the reduction in close relationships available to students at home, at church, or in their communities has been echoed in the schools. In the past 20 years, schools have become much larger, with corresponding increases in bureaucratization and a concomitant impersonal formality. Teachers are less accessible—often because they have to be out of the building by a certain time at the end of the day for security's sake. Instructional methods, too, emphasize impersonality. Current estimates are that over 85 percent of the instruction in schools consists of lectures, seatwork, or competition, where students are isolated from one another, and forbidden to interact.

All of these facets of school life ignore the importance of relationships with other children and adolescents for *constructive* socialization and healthy cognitive and social development. Constructive peer relationships, characterized by caring, commitment, support, and encouragement, are just as important as constructive adult-child relationships for the development of healthy, productive adults. In most schools, however, legitimate peer interaction among students has been limited to extracurricular activities—and these are usually run by the same small groups of students who run everything in a school.

There are a number of special issues concerning school districts that require intensive, collaborative interaction among *all* students, such as:

1. Both desegregation and mainstreaming of handicapped children require building constructive relationships among heterogeneous students who may have initial prejudices and negative attitudes toward one another.
2. The prevention of delinquency, drug abuse, and other socially dysfunctional behaviors requires building positive relationships among high-risk children and those adolescents and peers who have more constructive attitudes and behavior patterns.

At a time when being able to interact effectively with other people is so vital in marriages, in families, on jobs, and in committees, schools insist that students don't talk to each other, don't work together, don't pay attention to or care about the work of other students — students are encouraged not to care about other students' learning in the classroom.

In our schools we can see to it that all of our students work to:

1. Achieve the mastery of facts, information, and theories they are taught in school.
2. Develop critical thinking competencies and the use of higher level reasoning strategies.
3. Develop positive attitudes toward subject areas, such as math and science, so that students are motivated to study these subjects and to learn more about them. Those who have special aptitudes must be qualified to take advanced training, so they can possibly enter careers related to science and math.
4. Acquire the ability to use their knowledge and resources in collaborative activities with other people in their careers, families, communities, and the larger society.
5. Acquire, insofar as we can help them to in the school setting, the psychological health and well-being required to participate effectively in our society.

Whether learning situations are structured competitively, individualistically, or cooperatively has a considerable impact on the achievement of school aims, but it probably rests on the appropriate use of the three modes. We believe, however, that cooperative learning has a special function in reinforcing these general aims concerned with the specific problems we have raised. We will discuss this relevance in some detail, as well as the research confirming our beliefs in the next chapter. But first, we'd like to explain what we mean by "competitive," "individualistic," and "cooperative" learning.

The Basic Elements of Cooperative Learning

What precisely is this mode of learning so many people are interested in pursuing? It sounds simple enough, true, but many practitioners who believe that they are using cooperative learning are, in fact, missing its essence. There is a crucial difference between putting students into groups to learn and in structuring cooperative interdependence among students.

Cooperation is *not* having students sit side-by-side at the same table to talk with each other as they do their individual assignments.

Cooperation is *not* having students do a task with instructions that those who finish first are to help the slower students.

Cooperation is *not* assigning a report to a group of students wherein one student does all the work and the others put their names on the product, as well.

Cooperation is much more than being physically near other students, discussing material with other students, helping other students or sharing material among students, although each of these is important in cooperative learning. Here's what cooperative learning is, as we see it.

There are four basic elements that must be included for small group learning to be truly cooperative.

The first is *positive interdependence*. This may be achieved through mutual goals (goal interdependence); divisions of labor (task interdependence); dividing materials, resources, or information among group members (resource interdependence); assigning students differing roles (role interdependence); and by giving joint rewards (reward interdependence). In order for a learning situation to be cooperative, students must perceive that they are positively interdependent with other members of their learning group.

Second, cooperative learning requires *face-to-face* interaction among students. There is no magic in positive interdependence in and of itself. It is the interaction patterns and verbal interchange among students promoted by the positive interdependence that affect education outcomes.

The third basic element of cooperative learning is *individual accountability* for mastering the assigned material. The purpose of a learning situation is to maximize the achievement of each individual student. Determining the level of mastery of each student is necessary so students can provide appropriate support and assistance to one another.

Finally, cooperative learning requires that students appropriately use *interpersonal and small-group skills*. Obviously, placing socially unskilled students in a learning group and telling them to cooperate will not be successful. Students must be taught the social skills needed for collaboration and they must be motivated to use them. Students must also be given the time and procedures for analyzing how well their learning groups are functioning and the extent to which students are employing their social skills to help all group members to achieve and to maintain effective working relationships within the group.

The Differences Between Traditional Group Learning and Cooperative Learning

There are a number of differences between the typical use of classroom learning groups and cooperative learning groups. These differences (summarized in Figure 1) are:

1. Cooperative learning groups are based on *positive interdependence* among group members, where goals are structured so that students need to be concerned about performance of *all* group members as well as their own.

2. In cooperative learning groups, there is a clear *individual accountability* where every student's mastery of the assigned material is assessed, each student is given feedback on his or her progress, and the group is given feedback on how each member is progressing so that the other groups' members know who to help and encourage. In traditional learning groups, individual students are not often held individually accountable for providing their share of the group's work and, occasionally, students will "hitchhike" on the work of others.

3. In cooperative learning groups, the membership is typically heterogeneous in ability and personal characteristics, while traditional learning groups are often homogeneous in membership.

4. In cooperative learning groups, all members share responsibility for performing leadership actions in the group. In traditional learning groups, a leader is often appointed and put in charge of the group.

5. In cooperative learning groups, responsibility for each other's learning is shared. Group members are expected to provide help and encouragement to each other in order to ensure that all members do the assigned work. In traditional learning groups, members are seldom held responsible for each other's learning.

6. In cooperative learning groups, the goals focus on bringing each member's learning to the maximum *and* on maintaining good working relationships among members. In traditional classroom learning groups, students most often focus only on completing the assignment.

7. In cooperative learning groups, the social skills students need in order to work collaboratively (such as leadership, ability to communicate, to trust one another, and to manage conflict) are directly taught. In traditional classroom learning groups, interpersonal and small-group skills are assumed—most often mistakenly.

8. When cooperative learning groups are used, the teacher observes the groups, analyzes the problems they have working together, and gives feedback to each group on how well they are managing the group task. Teacher observation and intervention seldom take place in traditional learning groups.
9. In cooperative learning, the teacher structures procedures for groups to "process" how effectively they are working, while no attention is given, in traditional group learning situations, to the way the group is working—or not working.

Figure 1. What Is the Difference?

Cooperative Learning Groups	Traditional Learning Groups
Positive interdependence	No interdependence
Individual accountability	No individual accountability
Heterogeneous	Homogeneous
Shared leadership	One appointed leader
Shared responsibility for each other	Responsibility only for self
Task and maintenance emphasized	Only task emphasized
Social skills directly taught	Social skills assumed and ignored
Teacher observes and intervenes	Teacher ignores group functioning
Groups process their effectiveness	No group processing

Conclusion

There is much that is disturbing in our society and, while we cannot redress all the negatives that affect our students, we can see to it that the schools do not exacerbate their problems.

We believe that the extensive and inappropriate overuse of competitive and individualistic instructional methods in our schools probably *does* reinforce some difficulties students encounter outside of school. Further, we believe that such practices do not adequately prepare students for the kinds of cooperative efforts that will be expected of them in their future work and home lives. The time has come to structure life in schools in ways that are: (1) congruent with the future lives of our students, and (2) congruent with research on instructional methods.

The set of strategies we support is more than simply a better way to work with students in a classroom. Whether students work together or alone in schools is more serious than that. We cannot, as a country, afford to have a significant number of students who are alienated, left out, disconnected from their peers. We cannot afford to graduate large numbers of students with little or no ability to interact effectively with others—a prime requisite in the world of work. And we cannot afford to teach students in an environment where they will not learn as much as they could.

Despite the importance we and others attach to cooperative learning experiences, there are critics who challenge its use, who question the validity of the claims of advocates. In the next chapter, therefore, we shall review the research that supports cooperative learning and we shall indicate briefly some of the problem areas in our society—and in education—where we believe cooperative learning would be an appropriate remedy.

2

Relevance of Research on Cooperative Learning

Cooperative learning is not a new idea—it is as old as humankind. The capacity to work cooperatively has been a major contributor to the survival of our species. Throughout human history, it has been those individuals who could organize and coordinate their efforts to achieve a common purpose that have been most successful in virtually any human endeavor. This is as true of joining with one's fellows to hunt or to raise a barn as it is of space exploration.

Certainly, the use of cooperative learning and education procedures is not new to American education. There have been periods in which cooperative learning had strong advocates and was widely used to promote the educational goals of that time.

One of the most successful advocates of cooperative learning was Colonel Francis Parker. In the last three decades of the 19th century, Colonel Parker brought to his advocacy of cooperative learning enthusiasm, idealism, practicality, and an intense devotion to freedom, democracy, and individuality in the public schools. His fame and success rested on the vivid and regenerating spirit he brought into the schoolroom and on his power to create a classroom atmosphere that was truly cooperative and democratic. When he was superintendent of the public schools in Quincy, Massachusetts (1875-1880), more than 30,000 visitors a year came to examine his use of cooperative learning procedures (Campbell, 1965). Parker's instructional methods of promoting cooperation among students dominated American education through the turn of the century.

Following Parker, John Dewey promoted the use of cooperative learning groups as part of his famous project method in instruction. In the late 1930s, however, interpersonal competition began to be emphasized in public schools.

In the 1940s, Morton Deutsch, building on the theorizing of Kurt Lewin, proposed a theory of cooperative and competitive situations that has served as the primary foundation on which subsequent research on and discussion of cooperative learning has been based. Our own work is directly based on the research of Deutsch.

Several groups of researchers and practitioners scattered throughout the United States and Canada and in several other countries are engaged in the study and implementation of cooperative learning environments and procedures. At Johns Hopkins University, the work on cooperative learning initiated by David Devries and Keith Edwards is being extended by Robert Slavin and his colleagues. Elliot Aronson, University of California at Santa Cruz, has developed a "jigsaw" procedure for using curriculum materials in order to encourage cooperative learning.

Others involved in studying and implementing cooperative learning procedures include Shlomo Sharan and Rachael Lazarowitz at Tel-Aviv University, Israel; Spencer Kagan at the University of California, Riverside; Gayle Hughes and her colleagues in the Department of Cooperation, Saskatchewan, Canada; Egil Hjertaker and his colleagues in Bagen, Norway, and many more (see Chapter 6).

Results of this research are of great significance in relation to the problems we discussed in Chapter 1. They indicate that cooperative learning can contribute to many of the goals for improvement we cited. Following are brief descriptions of research results.

Achievement

Since the 1920s, there has been a great deal of research on the relative effects of cooperative, competitive, and individualistic efforts on achievement and productivity, including our own 20 research studies (Johnson and Johnson, 1983). Social scientists have disagreed, however, as to the conclusions that might be drawn from the literature.

In order to resolve the controversies resulting from the various reviews on social interdependence and achievement, we conducted a meta-analysis of all the studies that had been conducted in the area (Johnson, Maruyama, Johnson, Nelson, and Skon, 1981). We reviewed 122 studies conducted between 1924 and 1981. Three methods of meta-analysis were used: voting method, effect-size method, and z-score method. Results indicate that cooperative learning experiences tend to promote higher achievement than do competitive and individualistic learning experiences. These results hold for all age levels, for all subject areas, and for tasks involving concept attainment, verbal problem solving, categorization, spatial problem solving, retention and memory, motor performance, and guessing-judging-predicting. For rote-decoding and correcting tasks, cooperation seems to be equally as effective as competitive and individualistic learning procedures.

Simply knowing that cooperative learning situations tend to promote higher achievement than do competitive, individualistic, or "traditional" learning situations is not enough. Why is cooperation more effective in promoting achievement? We and our colleagues have conducted an extensive research program aimed at identifying the factors that contribute to the effectiveness of cooperative learning (Johnson and Johnson, 1983) with the following results:

1. The type of learning task assigned does not seem to matter a great deal. Currently, there is no type of learning task on which cooperative efforts are *less* effective than are competitive or individualistic efforts. On most tasks (and especially the more important learning tasks, such as concept attainment, verbal problem solving, categorization, spatial problem solving, retention and memory, motor learning, guessing-judging-predicting), cooperative efforts are usually more effective in promoting achievement.

2. The discussion process in cooperative learning groups promotes the discovery and development of higher quality cognitive strategies for learning than does the individual reasoning found in competitive and individualistic learning situations.

3. Involved participation in cooperative learning groups inevitably produces conflicts among the ideas, opinions, conclusions, theories, and information of members. When managed skillfully, such controversies promote increased motivation to achieve, higher achievement and retention of the learned material, and greater depth of understanding.

4. The discussion among students within cooperative learning situations promotes more frequent oral repetition of information; stating of new information; and explaining, integrating, and providing rationales. Such oral rehearsal of information is necessary for the

storage of information into the memory; it promotes long-term retention of the information; and it generally increases achievement.

5. Within cooperative learning groups, there tend to be considerable peer regulation, feedback, support, and encouragement of learning. Such peer academic support is unavailable in competitive and individualistic learning situations.

6. The exchange of ideas among students from high, medium, and low achievement levels, handicapped or not, and different ethnic backgrounds enriches their learning experiences. Cooperative learning groups seem to be nourished by heterogeneity among group members as students accommodate themselves to each other's perspectives.

7. The liking students develop for each other when they work collaboratively tends to increase their motivation to learn and to encourage each other to achieve. The motivation to learn in order to fulfill one's responsibilities to one's peers is not a part of individualistic and competitive learning situations.

Currently, our students believe that a learning task is completed when they have an answer in every blank in a worksheet. Sustained effort to comprehend material deeply seems to be rare. The Japanese, on the other hand, view academic success as a matter of disciplined, enduring effort aimed at achieving *satori*, or the sudden flash of enlightenment that comes after long, intensive, but successful effort. We believe the achievement of *satori* is much more likely after a discussion in cooperative learning groups than after working alone, competitively, or individually to complete an assignment.

Critical Thinking Competencies

In many subject areas related to science and technology, the teaching of facts and theories is considered to be secondary to the teaching of critical thinking and the use of higher level reasoning strategies. The aim of science education, for example, has been to develop individuals "who can sort sense from nonsense," or who have the critical thinking abilities of grasping information, examining it, evaluating it for soundness, and applying it appropriately. Cooperative learning promotes the use of higher reasoning strategies and greater critical thinking competencies more than do competitive and individualistic learning strategies (Johnson and Johnson, 1983).

Attitudes Toward Subject Areas

Our research indicates that cooperative learning experiences, compared with competitive and individualistic ones, promote more positive attitudes toward both the subject area and the instructional experience, as well as more continuing motivation to learn more about the subject area being studied (Johnson and Johnson, 1983).

Collaborative Competencies

Schooling is future-oriented in the sense that the instruction taking place is primarily aimed at preparing students for career and adult responsibilities. And the assumption is made that students will be able to apply successfully what they learn in school to career, family, community, and social settings. The industrial strategy of Japan is a good illustration of this principle. Japanese management has been quoted as stating that the superiority of the Japanese industrial system is not based on the fact that their workers are more intelligent than are the workers of other countries, but that their workers are better able to work in harmony and cooperation with each other, a goal that major U.S. companies have been working toward for years. Our research shows that there is considerable evidence that students working together in cooperative learning groups master collaborative competencies at a higher level than do students studying competitively or individualistically (Johnson and Johnson, 1983).

Psychological Health

When students leave school, we would hope that they would have the psychological health and stability required to build and maintain career, family, and community relationships, to establish a basic and meaningful interdependence with other people, and to participate effectively in our society. Our studies (Johnson and Johnson, 1983) indicate that cooperativeness is positively related to a number of indices of psychological health, namely: emotional maturity, well-adjusted social relations, strong personal identity, and basic trust in and optimism about people. Competitiveness seems also to be related to a number of indices of psychological health, while individualistic attitudes tend to be related to a number of indices of psychological pathology, emotional immaturity, social maladjustment, delinquency, self-alienation, and self-rejection. To the degree that schools can contribute to a student's psychological well-being, they should be organized to reinforce those traits and tendencies that promote it.

Socialization and Development

In our experience, cooperative learning does promote constructive socialization. For the past several years we have conducted a program of research aimed at studying the relative impact of cooperative, competitive, and individualistic learning experiences on aspects of socialization and development. This program is based on the theoretical model summarized in Figure 2.

We posited that there is a process of acceptance or rejection among students based on the type of student-student interaction pattern promoted by the instructional methods used by teachers. Acceptance tends to result from cooperative learning experiences; rejection is the result of competitive and individualistic learning experiences (Johnson, Johnson, and Maruyama, 1983). More specifically, cooperative learning experiences tend to lead to:

1. Promotive interaction
2. Feelings of psychological acceptance
3. Accurate perspective-taking
4. Differentiated, dynamic, and realistic views of collaborators and one's self
5. Psychological success
6. Basic self-acceptance and high self-esteem
7. Liking for other students
8. Expectations of rewarding, pleasant, and enjoyable future interactions with collaborators.

Liking for Classmates

Cooperative learning experiences, compared with competitive, individualistic, and "traditional" ones, promote considerable more liking among students (Johnson and Johnson, 1983; Johnson, Johnson, and Maruyama, 1983). This is true regardless of differences in ability level, sex, handicapping conditions, ethnic membership, social class differences, or task orientation. Students who collaborate on their studies develop considerable commitment and caring for each other no matter what their initial impressions of and attitudes toward each other were. We have conducted a series of studies on mainstreaming, ethnic integration, and relationships between males and females to determine whether

Figure 2. Social Judgment Process.

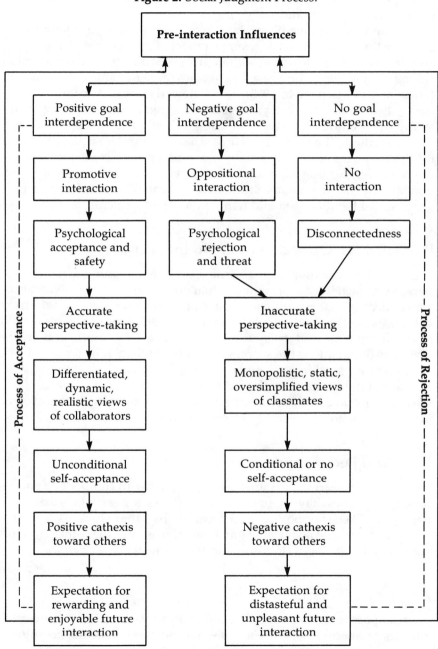

there are limits to the impact of cooperation on liking among students. So far none have been found.

In addition to our own research we recently completed a meta-analysis of all existing research on the relative impact of cooperative, competitive, and individualistic learning experiences on interpersonal attraction among homogeneous and heterogeneous samples of students (Johnson, Johnson, and Maruyama, 1983). We reviewed 98 studies conducted between 1944 and 1982 that yielded 251 findings. Three types of meta-analysis procedures were used: voting-method, effect-size method, and z-score method. The results of all three analyses provide strong validation for the proposition that cooperative, compared with competitive or individualistic, learning experiences promote greater interpersonal attraction among homogeneous students, students from different ethnic groups, and handicapped and nonhandicapped students.

Promotive vs. Oppositional or No Interaction

One reason why cooperative learning experiences promote more interpersonal attraction among students than do competitive or individualistic experiences is that within cooperative situations students benefit from helping each other learn, while in competitive situations students benefit from obstructing and frustrating each other's learning, and in individualistic situations the success or failure of others is irrelevant. There is, therefore, considerably more helping, encouraging, tutoring, and assisting among students (including cross-ethnic and cross-handicap relationships) in cooperative than in competitive or individualistic learning situations (Johnson and Johnson, 1983).

Perceived Peer Support and Acceptance

Cooperative learning experiences, compared with competitive and individualistic ones, have been found to result in stronger beliefs that one is personally liked, supported, and accepted by other students, and that other students care about how much one learns, and that other students want to help one learn (Johnson and Johnson, 1983).

Accuracy of Perspective-Taking

Social perspective-taking is the ability to understand how a situation appears to another person and how that person is reacting cognitively and emotionally to the situation. The opposite of perspective-taking is egocentrism, the embeddedness in one's own viewpoint to the extent that one is unaware of other points of view and of the limitations of one's perspectives. Cooperative learning experiences tend to promote greater cognitive and affective perspective-taking than do competitive or individualistic learning experiences (Johnson and Johnson, 1983).

Differentiation of Views of Others

Stereotypes usually focus on only a few characteristics of a person and remain static (not changing from situation to situation). Views of other students alternatively may become differentiated (taking into account many different characteristics), dynamic (being modified from situation to situation), and realistic. Cooperative learning experiences tend to promote more differentiated, dynamic, and realistic views (and therefore less stereotyped and static views) of other students (including handicapped peers and students from different ethnic groups) than do competitive and individualistic learning experiences (Johnson and Johnson, 1983).

Self-Esteem

Cooperative learning experiences, compared with competitive and individualistic ones, promote higher levels of self-esteem (Johnson and Johnson, 1983). Cooperativeness, furthermore, tends to be related to basic self-acceptance; competitiveness tends to be related to contingent self-acceptance; and individualistic attitudes tend to be related to basic self-rejection.

Expectations Toward Future Interaction

Cooperative learning experiences tend to promote expectations toward more rewarding and enjoyable future interaction among students (Johnson and Johnson, 1983).

Relationships with School Personnel

Cooperative learning experiences not only affect relationships with other students, they also affect relationships with adults in the school. Students participating in cooperative learning experiences, compared with students participating in competitive and individualistic learning experiences, like the teacher better and perceive the teacher as being more supportive and accepting academically and personally (Johnson and Johnson, 1983).

Summary

Achievement will be higher when learning situations are structured cooperatively rather than competitively or individualistically. Cooperative learning experiences, furthermore, promote greater competencies in critical thinking, more positive attitudes toward the subject areas studied, greater competencies in working collaboratively with others, greater psychological health, and greater perceptions of the grading system as being fair. The implications of these results for teachers are:

1. Cooperative learning procedures may be used successfully with any type of academic task, although the greater the conceptual learning required the greater will tend to be the efficacy of cooperation.
2. Whenever possible, cooperative groups should be structured so that controversy and academic disagreements among group members is possible and managed constructively.
3. Students should be encouraged to keep each other on task and discuss the assigned material in ways that ensure elaborative rehearsal and the use of higher level learning strategies.
4. Students should be encouraged to support each other's efforts to achieve, regulate each other's task-related efforts, provide each other with feedback, and ensure that all group members are verbally involved in the learning process.
5. As a rule, cooperative groups should contain low, medium, and high ability students to help promote discussion, peer teaching, and justification of answers.
6. Positive relationships among group members should be encouraged.

Cooperative learning experiences, where students work together to maximize each other's achievement, tend also to promote positive relationships and a process of acceptance among students, thereby making an important contribution to the solution of the socialization crisis. More specifically, educators who wish to promote constructive relationships among students will wish to (Johnson and Johnson, 1982c):

1. Structure cooperative situations in which children and adolescents work with peers to achieve a common goal

2. Emphasize joint rather than individual products whenever possible
3. Directly teach the interpersonal skills needed to build and maintain collaborative relationships with peers
4. Give children and adolescents meaningful responsibility for the well-being and success of their peers
5. Encourage the feelings of support, acceptance, concern, and commitment that are part of collaborative situations
6. Hold children and adolescents accountable for fulfilling their obligations and responsibilities to their collaborators and give them mutual authority over each other
7. Ensure that children experience success in a cooperative group setting.

All of these strategies can be accomplished, but it will take some training of students and of teachers, plus strong support from school administrators. How schools can go about using cooperative learning is the subject of the following chapters.

3 Implementing Cooperative Learning

Having discussed what cooperative learning is and how it differs from competitive and individualistic learning, and the considerable research validating its effectiveness compared with competitive and individualistic learning, the next issue is how cooperative learning situations are effectively structured. What do teachers need to know in order to use cooperative learning groups effectively? One thing is clear. A prepackaged program will not work. Good teachers would feel too constricted, and average teachers would use it for awhile and then drop it. What is needed is a general procedure, specific enough to give teachers guidance, but flexible enough for teachers to adapt it to their specific teaching situations.

The essence of cooperative learning is *positive interdependence*—students recognize that "we are in this together, sink or swim." In addition, cooperative learning situations are characterized by *individual accountability*, where every student is accountable for both learning the assigned material and helping other group members learn; *face-to-face interaction* among students; and students appropriately using *interpersonal and group skills*.

There is more to the teacher's role in

structuring cooperative learning situations, however, than structuring cooperation among students. The teacher's role includes five major sets of strategies:

1. Clearly specifying the objectives for the lesson
2. Making decisions about placing students in learning groups before the lesson is taught
3. Clearly explaining the task, goal structure, and learning activity to the students
4. Monitoring the effectiveness of the cooperative learning groups and intervening to provide task assistance (such as answering questions and teaching task skills) or to increase students' interpersonal and group skills
5. Evaluating students' achievement and helping students discuss how well they collaborated with each other.

The following 18 steps elaborate these strategies and detail a procedure for structuring cooperative learning. Specific examples of lessons may be found in Chasnoff (1979), Lyons (1980), and Roy (1982). There are also two films available demonstrating the use of cooperative learning procedures *(Belonging, Circles of Learning)*.

Objectives

1. *Specifying Instructional Objectives*

There are two types of objectives that a teacher needs to specify before the lesson begins. The *academic objective* needs to be specified at the correct level for the students and matched to the right level of instruction according to a conceptual or task analysis. The *collaborative skills objective* details what collaborative skills are going to be emphasized during the lesson.

Decisions

2. *Deciding on the Size of the Group*

Once the lesson objectives are clear, the teacher must decide which size of learning group is optimal. Cooperative learning groups tend to range in size from two to six. A number of factors should be considered in selecting the size of a cooperative learning group:

a. As the size of the group increases, the range of abilities, expertise, skills, and number of minds available for acquiring and processing information increase. The more group members you have, the more chance to have someone who has special knowledge helpful to the group and the more willing hands and talents are available to do the task.

b. The larger the group, however, the more skillful group members must be in providing everyone with a chance to speak, coordinating the actions of group members, reaching consensus, ensuring elaboration of the material being learned, and keeping all members on task. Very few students have the collaborative skills needed for effective group functioning and, therefore, the skills have to be initially taught.

c. The materials available or the specific nature of the task may dictate group size.

d. The shorter the period of time available, the smaller the learning group should be. Smaller groups will be more effective because they take less time to get organized, they operate faster, and there is more "air time" per member.

Our best advice to beginning teachers is to start with pairs or threesomes. As students become more experienced and skillful, they will be able to manage larger groups. Six may be the upper limit for a cooperative learning group in most schools—more members would be too large even for *very* skillful members. In one classroom we recently observed the teacher had divided the class into "committees" of eight. In the typical committee some students were being left out, others were passive, and some were engaged in a conversation with only one or two other members. Cooperative learning groups need to be small enough for everyone to engage in mutual discussion while achieving the group's goals. So be cautious about group size. Some students will not be ready for a group as large as four.

3. *Assigning Students to Groups*

There are five basic questions teachers often ask about assigning students to groups:

a. Should students be placed in learning groups homogeneous or heterogeneous in member ability? There are times when cooperative homogeneous learning groups may be used to master specific skills or to achieve certain instructional objectives. Generally, however, we recommend that teachers emphasize heterogeneity of students—placing high-, medium-, and low-ability students within the same learning group. More elaborative thinking, more frequent giving and receiving of explanations, and greater perspective in discussing material seem to occur in heterogeneous groups, all of which increase the depth of understanding, the quality of reasoning, and the accuracy of long-term retention.

b. Should non-task-oriented students be placed in learning groups with task-oriented peers or be separated? To keep such students on task, it often helps to place them in a cooperative learning group with task-oriented peers.

c. Should students select who they want to work with or should the teacher assign groups? Having students select their own groups is often not very successful. Student-selected groups often are homogeneous with high-achieving students working with other high-achieving students, white students working with other white students, minority students working with other minority students, and males working with other males. Often there is less on-task behavior in student-selected than in teacher-selected groups. A useful modification of the "select your own group" method is to have students list who they would like to work with and then place them in a learning group with one person they choose plus a few more students selected by the teacher. Teacher-made groups often have the best mix since teachers can put together optimal combinations of students. There are many ways teachers may assign students to learning groups. Some additional ways are:

1) Ask students to list three peers with whom they would like to work. Identify the isolated students who are not chosen by any other classmates. Then build a group of skillful and supportive students around each isolated child.

2) Randomly assign students by having them count off and placing the one's together, the two's together, and so forth. If groups of three are desired in a class of 30, have the students count off by tens.

3) How do desegregation and mainstreaming relate to how teachers assign students to learning groups? In order to build constructive relationships between majority and minority students, between handicapped and nonhandicapped students, and even between male and female students, use heterogeneous cooperative learning groups with a variety of students within each learning group.

d. How long should the groups stay together? For the length of the instructional unit? Actually, there is no formula or simple answer to this question. Some teachers keep cooperative learning groups together for an entire year or semester. Other teachers change group membership often. An elementary school setting allows students to be in several different learning groups during the day. Our best advice is to allow groups to remain stable long enough for them to be successful. Breaking up groups that are having trouble functioning effectively is often counterproductive, as the students do not learn the skills they need to resolve problems in collaborating with each other.

There is merit in having students work with everyone in their class during a semester or school year. Building a strong positive feeling of collaboration across an entire class and giving students opportunities to practice the skills needed to begin new groups can add much to the learning experience. Finally, never underestimate the power of heterogeneous cooperative learning groups in promoting high quality, rich, and involved learning.

4. *Arranging the Room*

How the teacher arranges the room is a symbolic message of what is appropriate behavior, and it can facilitate the learning groups within the classroom. The group members should sit in a circle and be close enough to each other to communicate effectively without disrupting the other learning groups, and the teacher should have a clear access lane to every group.

One common mistake that teachers make in arranging a room is to place students at a rectangular table where they cannot have eye contact with all the other members; another is to place a number of desks together, which places students too far apart to quietly communicate with each other. Within each learning group students need to be able to see all relevant task materials, see each other, converse with each other without raising their voices, and exchange ideas and materials in a comfortable atmosphere. The groups need to be far enough apart so that they do not interfere with each other's learning.

5. *Planning the Instructional Materials to Promote Interdependence*

The way teachers structure the materials to be used during a lesson can lead both to effective academic learning and positive interdependence among group members. When a group is mature and experienced and group members have a high level of collaborative skills, the teacher may not have to arrange materials in any specific way. When a group is new or when members are not very skilled, however, teachers may wish to distribute materials in carefully planned ways to communicate that the assignment is to be a joint (not an individual) effort and that the students are in a "sink or swim together" learning situation. Three ways of doing so are:

a. *Materials Interdependence:* Give only one copy of the materials to the group. The students will then have to work together in order to be successful. This is especially effective the first few times the group meets. After students are accustomed to collaborating with each other, teachers will wish each student to have an individual copy of the materials.

b. *Information Interdependence:* Group members may each be given different books or resource materials to be synthesized. Or the materials may be arranged like a jigsaw puzzle so that each student has part of the materials needed to complete the task (Aronson, and others, 1978). Such procedures require that every member participate in order for the group to be successful.

c. *Interdependence with Other Groups:* Materials may be structured into a tournament format with intergroup competition as the basis to promote a perception of interdependence among group members. Such a procedure was introduced by DeVries and Edwards (1973) and extended by Slavin (1974). In the teams-games-tournament format, students are divided into heterogeneous cooperative learning teams to prepare members for a tournament in which they compete with the other teams. During the intergroup competition the students individually compete against members of about the same ability level from other teams. The team whose members do the best in the competition is pronounced the winner.

All of these procedures may not be needed simultaneously. They are alternative methods of ensuring that students perceive that they must work together and behave collaboratively to succeed in the learning situation.

6. *Assigning Roles to Ensure Interdependence*

Cooperative interdependence may also be arranged through the assignment of complementary and interconnected roles to group members. An example is a science lesson we helped develop. Each group member is assigned a responsibility that must be fulfilled if the group is to function. For example, the group should have a *summarizer-checker* to make sure everyone in the group understands what is being learned; a *researcher-runner* to get needed materials for the group and to communicate with the other learning groups and the teacher; a *recorder* to write down the group's decisions and to edit the group's report; an *encourager* to reinforce members' contributions; and an *observer* to keep track of how well the group is collaborating. Assigning such roles is an effective method of teaching students collaborative skills.

With these decisions made and the appropriate materials prepared, the teacher is ready to explain the instructional task and the cooperative goal structure to the class. The less experience the students have in working in cooperative learning groups, the more important it is that teachers explain carefully what cooperation is.

7. *Explaining the Academic Task*

Teachers should consider several aspects of explaining an academic assignment to students:

a. Set the task so that students are clear about the assignment. Most teachers have considerable practice with this. Instructions that are clear and specific are crucial in warding off student frustration. One advantage of cooperative learning groups is that these students can handle more ambiguous tasks (when appropriate) than can students working alone. In cooperative learning groups students who do not understand what they are to do will ask their group for clarification before asking the teacher.

b. Explain the objectives of the lesson and relate the concepts and information to be studied to students' past experience and learning to ensure maximum transfer and retention. Explaining the intended outcomes of the lesson increases the likelihood that students will focus on the relevant concepts and information throughout the lesson.

c. Define relevant concepts, explain procedures students should follow, and give examples to help students understand what they are to learn and to do in completing the assignment. To promote positive transfer of learning, point out the critical elements that separate this lesson from past learnings.

d. Ask the class specific questions to check the students' understanding of the assignment. Such questioning ensures that thorough two-way communication exists, that the assignment has been given effectively, and that the students are ready to begin completing it.

8. *Structuring Positive Goal Interdependence*

Communicate to students that they have a group goal and must work collaboratively. We cannot overemphasize the importance of communicating to students that they are in a "sink or swim together" learning situation. In a cooperative learning group students must understand that they are responsible for learning the assigned material, making sure that all other group members learn the assigned material, and making sure that all other group members successfully complete the assignments, in that order. Teachers can do this in several ways:

a. Ask the group to produce a single product, report, or paper. Each group member should sign the paper to indicate that he or she agrees with the answers and can explain why the answers are appropriate. Each student must know the material. When a group is producing only one product it is especially important to stress individual accountability. Teachers may pick a student at random from each group to explain the rationale for their answers.

b. Provide group rewards. A group grade is one way to emphasize the necessity for collaboration. A spelling group where the group members work with each other during the week to make sure that all members know their words, so they can take the test individually, can be rewarded on the basis of the total number of words spelled correctly by all the members of the group. Math lessons can be structured so that students work in cooperative learning groups, take a test individually, receive an individual score, but are given bonus points on the basis of how many group members reach a preset level of excellence. Some teachers reward groups where all members reach a preset criterion of excellence with free-time or extra recess.

Positive interdependence creates peer encouragement and support for learning. Such positive peer pressure influences underachieving students to become academically involved. Members of cooperative learning groups should give two interrelated messages, "Do your work—we're counting on you!" and "How can I help you to do better?"

9. *Structuring Individual Accountability*

The purpose of a cooperative learning group is to enhance the learning of each member. A learning group is not truly cooperative if individual members let others do all the work. In order to ensure that all members learn and that groups know which members to provide with encouragement and help, teachers will need to assess frequently the level of performance of each group member—by giving practice tests, randomly selecting members to explain answers, having members edit each other's work, or by randomly picking one paper from the group to grade. These are only a few ways individual accountability can be structured.

10. *Structuring Intergroup Cooperation*

The positive outcomes found within a cooperative learning group can be extended throughout a whole class by structuring intergroup cooperation other than through the competitive tournament format. Bonus points may be given if all members of a class reach a preset criterion of excellence. When a group finishes its work, the teacher should encourage the members to help other groups complete the assignment.

11. *Explaining Criteria for Success*

Rather than grading on a curve, evaluation within cooperatively structured lessons needs to be based on criteria established for acceptable work. Thus, at the beginning of the lesson teachers should clearly explain the criteria by which the students' work will be evaluated. The criteria for success must be structured so that students may reach it without penalizing other students and so that groups may reach it without penalizing other groups.

For some learning groups, all members can be working to reach the same criteria. For other learning groups, different members may be evaluated according to different criteria. The criteria should be tailored to be challenging and realistic for each individual group member. In a spelling group, for example, some members may not be able to learn as many as 20 words, and the number of words for such students can be reduced accordingly.

Teachers may structure a second level of cooperation not only by keeping track of how well each group and its members are performing, but also by setting criteria for the whole class to reach. Thus, the number of words the total class spells correctly can be recorded from week to week with appropriate criteria being set to promote class-wide collaboration and encouragement. These criteria are important to give students information about what "doing well" means on assigned tasks, but they do not always have to be as formal as counting the number of correct answers. On some assignments, simply completing the task may be an adequate criterion for assessing the work of some students. For others, simply doing better this week than last week may be set as a criterion of excellence.

12. *Specifying Desired Behaviors*

The word cooperation has different connotations and uses. Teachers need to define cooperation operationally by specifying the behaviors that are appropriate and desirable within the learning groups. There are beginning behaviors, such as "stay with your group and do not wander around the room," "use quiet voices," "take turns," and "use each other's names." When groups begin to function more effectively, expected behaviors may include:

a. Have each member explain how to get the answer
b. Ask each member to relate what is being learned to previous learnings
c. Check to make sure everyone in the group understands the material and agrees with the answers the group has developed
d. Encourage everyone to participate
e. Listen accurately to what all group members are saying
f. Encourage each member to be persuaded by the logic of the answers proposed, not by group pressure; majority rule does not promote learning
g. Criticize ideas, not people.

The list of expected behaviors should not be too long. One or two behaviors is enough for a few lessons. Students need to know what behavior is appropriate and desirable within a cooperative learning group, but they should not be subjected to information overload.

Monitoring and Intervening

13. *Monitoring Students' Behavior*

The teacher's job begins in earnest when the cooperative learning groups start working. Resist that urge to get a cup of coffee or grade some papers. Just because the teacher places students in learning groups and instructs them to be cooperative does not mean that they will always do so. Therefore, much of the teacher's time should be spent in observing group members in order to see what problems they are having in completing the assignment and in working collaboratively. A variety of observation instruments and procedures that can be used for these purposes can be found in Johnson and Johnson (1975), Johnson and Johnson (1982), Chasnoff (1979), Lyons (1980), and Roy (1982).

Whenever possible, teachers should use a formal observation sheet to count the number of times they observe appropriate behaviors being used by students. The more concrete the data, the more useful it is to the teacher and to students. Teachers should not try to count too many different behaviors at one time, especially when they start formal observation. At first they may just record who talks in each group to get a participation pattern for the groups. Some help on observation can be found in a chapter describing systematic observation of cooperative groups in *Learning Together and Alone* (Johnson and Johnson, 1975). Our current list of behaviors (though rather long) includes: contributing ideas, asking questions, expressing feelings, actively listening, expressing support and acceptance (toward ideas), expressing warmth and liking (toward group members and group), encouraging all members to participate, summarizing, checking for understanding, relieving tension by joking, and giving direction to the group work.

We look for positive behaviors, which are to be praised when they are appropriately present and which are a cause for discussion when they are missing. It is also a good idea for the teacher to collect notes on specific student behaviors so that the frequency data is extended. Especially useful are skillful interchanges that can be shared with students later in the form of objective praise and perhaps with parents in conferences or telephone conversations.

Student observers can get even more extensive data on each group's functioning. For very young students the system must be kept very simple, perhaps only "Who talks?" Many teachers have had success with student observers, even in kindergarten.

One of the more important things the teacher can do is to make sure that the class is given adequate instructions (and perhaps practice) on gathering the observation data and sharing it with the group. The observer is in the best position to learn about the skills of working in a group. We remember one 1st-grade teacher who had a student who talked all the time (even to himself while working alone). He dominated any group he was in. When the teacher introduced student observers to the class she made the student an observer. (One important rule for observers is not to interfere in the task but to gather data without talking.) He gathered data on who talked and did a good job, noting that one student had done quite a bit of talking in the group while another had talked very little. The next day when he was back in the group and no longer the observer, he started to talk, clamped his hand over his mouth, and glanced at the new observer. He knew what behavior was being observed, and he didn't want to be the only one with marks for talking. The teacher said he may have listened for the first time all year. Thus the observer often benefits by learning about group skills.

Observers, moreover, often know quite a bit about the lesson. When teachers are worried about losing the lesson content, they can have the observer take the group through the material as a last review. Often important changes are made during this review.

It is not necessary to use student observers all the time, and we would not recommend their use until cooperative learning groups have been used a few times. In the beginning it is enough for teachers simply to structure the groups to be cooperative without worrying about structuring student observers, too. Whether student observers are used or not, however, teachers should always do some observing and spend time monitoring the groups. Sometimes a simple checklist is helpful in addition to a systematic observation form. Some questions to ask on the checklist might be: Are students practicing the specified behaviors, or not? Do they understand the task? Have they accepted the positive interdependence and the individual accountability? Are they working toward the criteria and are the criteria for success appropriate?

14. *Providing Task Assistance*

In monitoring the groups as they work, teachers will wish to clarify instructions, review important procedures and strategies for completing the assignment, answer questions, and teach task skills as necessary. In discussing the concepts and information to be learned, teachers should use the language or terms relevant to the learning. Instead of saying, "Yes, that is right," teachers might say something more specific to the assignment, such as, "Yes, that is one way to find the main idea of a paragraph." The use of specific statements reinforces the desired learning and promotes positive transfer.

15. *Intervening to Teach Collaborative Skills*

While monitoring the learning groups, teachers sometimes find students without the necessary collaborative skills and groups with problems in collaborating. In these cases the teacher may intervene to suggest more effective procedures for working together and more effective behaviors for students to engage in. Teachers may also wish to intervene and reinforce particularly effective and skillful behaviors as they are noticed. The teacher at times is a consultant to a group. When it is obvious that group members lack the necessary collaborative skills to cooperate with each other, the coordinator will want to intervene to help the members learn these skills. Collaborative skills, along with activities that may be used in teaching them, are covered in Johnson and Johnson (1982) and Johnson (1978, 1981).

Teachers should not intervene in the groups any more than is absolutely necessary. Most teachers are geared to jumping in and solving problems for students as they occur. With a little patience, we find that cooperative groups can often work their way through their own problems (task and maintenance) and acquire not only a solution, but also a method of solving similar problems in the future. Choosing when to intervene and when not to is part of the art of teaching, and teachers can usually trust their intuition. Even after intervening, teachers can turn the problem back to the group to solve. Many teachers intervene by having members set aside their task, pointing out the problem, and asking the group to come up with an adequate solution. The last thing teachers want is for the students to come running to the teacher with every problem.

For example, a 3rd-grade teacher noticed while passing out papers that one student was leaning back away from the other three group members. A moment later, the three students marched over to the teacher and complained that Johnny was under the table and wouldn't come out. "Make him come out!" they insisted (the teacher's role: police officer, judge, and executioner). The teacher told them that Johnny was a member of their group and asked what they had tried. The children were puzzled. "Yes, have you asked him to come out?" the teacher suggested. The group marched back, and the teacher continued passing out papers. A moment later the teacher glanced at their table and saw *no* heads above the table (which is one way to solve the problem). Shortly, four heads came struggling out from under the table, and the group (including Johnny) went back to work with great energy.

We don't know what happened under that table, but whatever it was, it was effective. What makes this story even more interesting is that the group received a 100 percent on the paper and later, when the teacher was at Johnny's desk, she noticed he had the paper clutched in his hand. The group had given Johnny the paper and he was taking it home. He confided to the teacher that this was the first time he could ever remember earning a 100 percent on anything in school. (If that was *your* record, you might slip under a few tables yourself.)

The best time to teach cooperative skills is when the students need them. It is important that the cooperative skills be taught in the appropriate context, or are practiced in that setting, because transfer of skill learning from one situation to another cannot be assumed. Students *learn about* cooperative skills when they are taught them, and *learn* cooperative skills when applying them in science, math, or English. The good news about cooperative skills is that they are taught and learned like any other skill (see Chapter 4). At a minimum:

a. Students need to recognize the need for the skill.
b. The skill must be defined clearly and specifically including what students should say when engaging in the skill.

c. Practice of the skill must be encouraged. Sometimes just the teacher standing nearby with a clipboard and pencil will be enough to promote student enactment of the skill.
d. Students should have the time and procedures to discuss how well they are using the skill.
e. Students should persevere in the practice until the skill is appropriately internalized. We never drop a skill, we only add on.

For older students (upper elementary school and above) the skills have been worked out and summarized in *Joining Together* (Johnson and F. Johnson, 1982) and *Reaching Out* (Johnson, 1981). For younger students, teachers may need to revise and rename cooperative skills. Some primary teachers use symbols like traffic signs with a "green light" encouraging participation, a "stop sign" meaning time to summarize, and "slippery when wet" meaning "Say that over again; I didn't quite understand."

Sometimes a more mechanistic structure is beneficial for young students. In one 1st-grade class, there were a number of students who liked to dominate and take over the group. One day, in frustration, the teacher formed groups and handed each group member five poker chips with a different color for each group member. The students were instructed to place one chip in a box every time they spoke while working on their worksheet. A student could not speak after all his or her chips were "spent." When all the chips were in the box, they could get their five colored chips back and start again. Several students were surprised when they discovered their five chips were the only ones in the box!

Teachers need only use these devices once or twice to get the message across. This technique was later used in a monthly principals' meeting. As the principals came in, each was handed several colored strips of paper. When they spoke . . .

Teaching cooperative skills is necessary for implementing cooperative learning groups into a classroom. We recommend that only a few skills be taught each semester. Most curriculum programs with cooperative learning groups written into them feature about five to eight cooperative skills for one year.

16. *Providing Closure to the Lesson*

At the end of the lesson, students should be able to summarize what they have learned and to understand where they will use it in future lessons. To reinforce student learning, teachers may wish to summarize the major points in the lesson, ask students to recall ideas or give samples, and answer any final questions they may have.

Evaluation and Processing

17. *Evaluating the Quality and Quantity of Students' Learning*

The product required from the lesson may be a report, a single set of answers agreed-upon by all group members, the average of individual examination scores, or the number of group members reaching a specific criterion. As we pointed out earlier, whatever the product, student learning needs to be evaluated by a criteria-referenced system. The procedures for setting up and using such an evaluation system are given in Johnson and Johnson (1975). In addition to an assessment on how well they are learning the assigned concepts and information, group members should also receive feedback on how effectively they collaborated. Some teachers give two grades, one for achievement and one for collaborative behavior.

18. *Assessing How Well the Group Functioned*

An old rule concerning observations of groups states that if you observe, you also must process those observations with the group. Processing need not occur in depth every day, but should happen often. Even if class time is limited, some time should be spent talking about how well the groups functioned today, what things were done well, and what things could be improved. Whole-class processing can include some feedback from the teacher (the principal observer) and some observations from members of the class. This can often include having a group share with the class an incident in their group and how they solved it. Names need not be used, but the feedback should be as specific as possible.

Groups new to processing often need an agenda, including specific questions each group member must address. A simple agenda might request each group to name two things they did well (and document them) and one thing they need to do even better, or would like to work harder on.

The time spent in discussing how well the group functioned is well spent, since each small group has two primary goals: (1) to accomplish the task successfully, and (2) to build and maintain constructive relationships in good working order for the next task. If a group is growing properly, it will become more and more effective. Often during the "working" part of the class period, students will be very task-oriented, and the "maintenance" of the group may suffer. During the processing time, however, the emphasis is on maintenance of the group, and the students leave the room ready for (a better?) tomorrow. If no processing is done, teachers may find the group's functioning decaying, and important relationships left undiscussed. Processing the functioning of the group needs to be taken as seriously as accomplishing the task. The two are very much related. Teachers often have students turn in a "process sheet" along with the paper required from the task assignment. Teachers will want to have a structured agenda or checklist for the groups to work with during the processing as inexperienced groups tend to say, "We did fine. Right? Right!" and not deal with any relevant issues.

Group processing should focus both on members' contributions to each other's learning and to the maintenance of effective working relationships among group members. In order to contribute to each other's learning, group members need to attend class, to have completed the necessary homework required for the group's work, and to have provided needed explanations and examples. Absenteeism and lack of preparation often demoralize other members. A productive group discussion is one in which members are present and prepared and there should be some peer accountability to be so.

On the other hand, learning groups are often exclusively task oriented and ignore the importance of maintaining effective working relationships among members. Group sessions should be enjoyable, lively, and pleasant. If no one is having fun, something is wrong. Problems should be brought up and solved, and there should be a continuing emphasis on improving the effectiveness of the group members in collaborating with each other.

Conclusions

These 18 aspects of structuring learning situations cooperatively blend together to make effective cooperative learning groups a reality in the classroom. They may be used in any subject area with any age student. Teachers who have mastered these strategies and integrated cooperative learning groups into their teaching often say, "Don't say it is easy!" There is a lot of pressure to teach like everyone else is teaching, to have students learn alone, and to not let students look on each other's papers. Students will not be accustomed to working together and are likely to have a competitive orientation. It isn't easy, but it is worth the effort.

Another bit of advice would be to start small and build. Pick a time in the school day when you are pretty sure it would work, plan carefully, and don't rush the process. Cooperative learning groups should evolve into a teacher's program rather than to become a part of every class on the first day.

The good news is that many of your students will do well immediately. While two groups may struggle because of a lack of group skills, five will do well. Celebrate the five and problem-solve with the two. Keep in mind that the students who are most difficult to integrate into groups are often the ones who need the peer support and positive peer pressure the most. Resist that advice you were given as a beginning teacher to isolate students who pester others or show that they lack interpersonal skills; instead, concentrate on integrating them into their peer group effectively. Other students often have the most powerful influence on isolated, alienated students. Such students cannot be allowed to plod through school disconnected, lonely, and bitter.

In addition, cooperative, supportive relationships are just as productive for adults as they are for students. Teachers are more effective when they have positive support from colleagues and can solve problems together. Teachers need to give some thought to establishing their own cooperative group as they implement cooperation in their classrooms (see Chapter 5).

It is also important to repeat that we would be disappointed if we visited a teacher's classroom and saw *only* cooperative learning groups. The data are clear. Cooperation should produce better results in school than having students work alone, individualisitically or competitively. Yet there is an important place for competitive and individualistic goal structures within the classroom. The major problems with competition and individualistic efforts result from overuse or inappropriate use.

In addition to cooperative skills, students need to learn how to compete for fun and enjoyment (win or lose) and how to work independently, following through on a task until completion. The natural place for competitive and individualistic efforts is under the umbrella of cooperation. The predominant use of cooperation reduces the anxiety and evaluation apprehension associated with competition. It also allows for using individualistically structured learning activities as part of a division of labor within cooperative tasks. But, most of all, students should learn how to work together and to give each other support in learning. Some teachers weave the three goal structures together: setting up individual responsibility (accountability to the group), peer teaching, competing as a light change of pace, and ending in a cooperative project. Thus, they do what schools should do—prepare students to interact effectively in cooperative, competitive, and individualistic structures.

4 Teaching Students Cooperative Skills

Students who have never been taught how to work effectively with others cannot be expected to do so. Thus, the first experience of many teachers who try structuring cooperative learning is that their students cannot collaborate with each other. Yet, it is within cooperative situations, where there is a task to complete, that social skills become most relevant and should ideally be taught. All students need to become skillful in communicating, building and maintaining trust, providing leadership, and managing conflicts (Johnson, 1978, 1981; Johnson and F. Johnson, 1982). Teaching collaborative skills becomes an important prerequisite for academic learning since achievement will improve as students become more effective in working with each other.

In this chapter we will review some of the assumptions that are vital to teaching cooperative skills, we will list and discuss some of the more basic skills, and then describe a model for teaching them.

Teaching Cooperative Skills: Assumptions

There are five assumptions underlying teaching students cooperative skills. *First*,

43

prior to teaching the skills a cooperative context must be structured. It makes little sense to teach students to communicate more effectively if they are expected to work alone without interacting with each other. Students who are competing want to "win," not learn the skills to resolve a conflict. Students' awareness of the need for collaborative skills is directly related to their being in cooperative learning situations. Implementing cooperative learning is vital to increasing students' collaborative competencies.

Second, cooperative skills have to be taught. Structuring lessons cooperatively is not enough. Students are not born with interpersonal and group skills, nor do they magically appear when the students need them. Learning how to interact effectively with others is no different than learning how to read, use a microscope, play a piano, or write a complete sentence. All skills are basically learned in the same way.

Third, peers are the key. While the teacher structures cooperative learning situations and initially defines the collaborative skills, it is other group members who determine whether the skills are practiced and internalized. After students know what the collaborative skills are and are encouraged to practice them in their cooperative learning groups, peer support and feedback will determine whether the skills are used appropriately and frequently enough for them to become natural and automatic actions. Peer feedback occurs subtly while the groups are working and directly in formal feedback sessions structured by the teacher.

The *fourth* assumption is that the peer pressure to learn cooperative skills must always be coupled with peer support for doing so. When there is an unskilled student within a cooperative learning group, group members need to know how to provide constructive support as well as pressure for the student to become more skilled. There will often be group members who want to dominate, some who are shy and afraid to participate, some who become angry when they give a wrong answer, and others who are embarrassed by having the group realize they do not understand the assigned material. The trick is to fashion an interdependent whole out of these disparate parts. Group members need to communicate both, "We want you to practice this collaborative skill," and "How can we help you do so?"

Finally, the *fifth* assumption is that the earlier students are taught cooperative skills, the better. There are procedures for kindergarten and even preschool teachers to use in teaching students collaborative skills (Chasnoff, 1979; Lyons, 1980; Roy, 1982). In elementary, secondary, and post-secondary settings, teachers should be involved in improving students' competencies in working collaboratively with each other. To inform engineers, managers, supervisors, or secretaries that they need to learn how to work more effectively with others is important, but a little late. Their education should have prepared them for joint efforts in adult careers and family life. There is a direct relation between schools demanding that students work alone without interacting with each other and the number of adults in our society who lack collaborative and interpersonal competence.

What Skills Need To Be Taught?

Numerous interpersonal skills affect the success of collaborative efforts (Johnson, 1981; Johnson and F. Johnson, 1982; Johnson and Johnson, 1975). Which cooperative skills teachers emphasize in their classes depend on which ones students have and have not mastered. As teachers observe and monitor their students working in cooperative learning groups, they will notice in which areas students lack important skills. Our list of required student behaviors may give teachers a starting point in examining how skillful their students are. There are four levels of cooperative skills:

1. Forming: The bottom-line skills needed to establish a functioning cooperative learning group.
2. Functioning: The skills needed to manage the group's activities in completing the task and in maintaining effective working relationships among members.
3. Formulating: The skills needed to build deeper level understanding of the material being studied, to stimulate the use of higher quality reasoning strategies, and to maximize mastery and retention of the assigned material.
4. Fermenting: The skills needed to stimulate reconceptualization of the material being studied, cognitive conflict, the search for more information, and the communication of the rationale behind one's conclusions.

Forming

Forming skills are those skills directed toward organizing the group and establishing minimum norms for appropriate behavior. Some of the more important behaviors in this category are:

1. Move into cooperative learning groups without undue noise and without bothering others: Work time in groups is a valuable com-

modity, and little time should be spent rearranging furniture and moving into learning groups. Students may need to practice the procedure for getting into groups several times before they become efficient in doing so.

2. Stay with the group: Moving around the room during group time is nonproductive both for the student doing it and other group members.

3. Use quiet voices: Cooperative learning groups do not need to be noisy and can learn to work very quietly. Some teachers assign one student in each group to make sure that everyone speaks softly.

4. Encourage everyone to participate: All group members need to share their ideas and materials and be part of the group's efforts to achieve. Taking turns is one way to formalize this.

5. Other necessary social skills include:
   a. Use names.
   b. Look at the speaker.
   c. No "put-downs."
   d. Keep one's hands (and feet) to one's self.

Functioning

The second level of cooperative skills are those involved in managing the group's efforts to complete their tasks and maintain effective working relationships among members. Some of these skills are:

1. Give direction to the group's work by:
   a. Stating and restating the purpose of the assignment
   b. Setting or calling attention to time limits
   c. Offering procedures on how most effectively to complete the assignment

2. Express support and acceptance both verbally and nonverbally through eye contact, enthusiasm, praise, and seeking others' ideas and conclusions

3. Ask for help or clarification of what is being said or done in the group

4. Offer to explain or clarify

5. Paraphrase and clarify another member's contributions

6. Energize the group when motivation is low by suggesting new ideas, by being enthusiastic through humor or

7. Describe one's feelings when appropriate.

The mixture of keeping members on task, finding effective and efficient work procedures, and fostering a pleasant and friendly work atmosphere is vital for effective leadership in cooperative learning groups.

Formulating

This set of skills is needed to provide the mental processes needed to build deeper understanding of the material being studied, to stimulate the use of higher quality reasoning strategies, and to ensure mastery and retention of the assigned material. Since the purpose of learning groups is to maximize the learning of all members, the following skills are specifically aimed at providing formal methods for processing the material being studied:

1. Summarize out loud what has just been read or discussed as completely as possible without referring to notes or to the original material. All important ideas and facts should be included in the summary. Every group member must summarize from memory often if learning is to be maximized.
2. Seek accuracy by correcting a member's summary, adding important information he or she did not include, and point out the ideas or facts that were summarized incorrectly.
3. Seek elaboration by asking other members to relate the material being learned to earlier material and to other things they know.
4. Seek clever ways to remember the important ideas and facts by using drawings, mental pictures, and other memory aids.
5. Demand vocalization to make overt the implicit reasoning process being used by other members and thus open to correction and discussion.
6. Ask other members to plan out loud how they would teach the material to another student. Planning how best to communicate the material can have important effects on the quality of reasoning strategies and retention.

Fermenting

Fermenting requires the skills needed to stimulate reconceptualization of the material being studied, cognitive conflict, the search for more information, and the communication of the rationale behind one's conclusions. Some of the most important aspects of learning take place when group members skillfully challenge each other's conclusions and reasoning (Johnson and R. Johnson, 1979). Academic controversies cause group members to dig deeper into the material, to assemble a rationale for their conclusions, to think more divergently about the issue, to find more information to support their positions, and to argue constructively about alternative solutions or decisions. Skills involved in academic controversies include:

1. Criticize ideas, not people.
2. Differentiate where there is disagreement within the learning group.
3. Integrate a number of different ideas into a single position.
4. Ask for justification of why the member's conclusion or answer is the correct or appropriate one.
5. Extend another member's answer or conclusion by adding further information or implications.
6. Probe by asking questions that lead to deeper understanding or analysis ("Would it work in this situation . . . ?" "What else makes you believe . . . ?").
7. Generate further answers by going beyond the first answer or conclusion and producing a number of plausible answers from which to choose an alternative.
8. Test reality by checking out the group's work with the instructions, available time, and other examples of reality.

Such skills keep group members motivated to go beyond the quick answer to the highest quality one. They are aimed at stimulating the thinking and intellectual curiosity of group members.

Briefly, teachers begin with *forming* skills to ensure that group members are present and oriented toward working with each other. The *functioning* skills then assist the group in operating smoothly and guiding constructive relationships among members. *Formulating* skills ensure that high-quality learning takes place within the group and that the members engage in the necessary cognitive processing. *Fermenting* skills are the most complex and the most difficult to master. They ensure that intellectual challenge and disagreement take place within the learning groups.

The above skills are discussed in terms of upper elementary, secondary, and post-secondary students. Primary and preschool students need simplified versions of the skills. It is important that teachers translate cooperative skills into language and images that their students can understand and identify with.

How To Teach Cooperative Skills

One of the most important aspects of conducting lessons structured cooperatively is to identify the students who are having difficulty in collaborating because of missing or underdeveloped social skills. The teacher's role of monitoring described in the last chapter highlights the importance of gathering data on students as they work and of intervening to encourage more appropriate behavior. Family background, role models, and the nature of the students' peer group all influence the development, or lack of development, of such skills. The exciting part of teaching students to be more effective collaborators is that the students not only gain a valuable set of skills for life, but have an excellent chance of raising their achievement as well.

To teach cooperative skills, the teacher should:

1. Ensure that students see the need for the skill.
2. Ensure that students understand what the skill is and when it should be used.
3. Set up practice situations and encourage mastery of the skill.
4. Ensure that students have the time and the needed procedures for discussing (and receiving feedback on) how well they are using the skill.
5. Ensure that students persevere in practicing the skill until the skill seems a natural action.

Step 1. Ensure that Students See the Need for the Skill

To be motivated to learn cooperative skills, students must believe that they are better off knowing, than not knowing, the skills. Teachers can promote students' awareness of the need for collaborative skills by:

1. Displaying in the room posters, bulletin boards, and other evidence that the teacher considers the skills to be important. It is often easy to see what is important in a classroom by looking at the walls, boards, and seating arrangements.
2. Communicating to students why mastering the skills is important. With many students, sharing information about the need for cooperative skills in career and family settings is enough. Other students may benefit from experiencing how the skills help them do better work.
3. Validating the importance of the skills by assigning a grade or giving a reward to groups whose members demonstrate competence in the skills. Many teachers give learning groups two grades: one for achievement and one for the appropriate use of targeted cooperative skills.

Although there are other ways to communicate the importance of cooperative skills—covering the walls, saying so, and rewarding the behavior get teachers off to a good start.

Step 2. Ensure that Students Understand What the Skill Is

To learn a skill, students must have a clear idea of what the skill is and how to perform it. There is little chance of being too concrete in defining cooperative skills. Every student needs to know what to say or do to perform the skill. Some strategies teachers can use in ensuring that students understand what a skill is and when it is to be appropriately used are:

1. Work with the students to generate specific phrases and behaviors that express the skill. "Do you agree?" asks for a "yes" or "no" answer and is, therefore, a much less effective encouraging question than is "How would you explain the answer?" The class may wish to list phrases the teacher should hear in each group as the teacher monitors the group's effectiveness. The list can then be prominently displayed for reference.
2. Demonstrating, modeling, and having students role-play the skill are all effective procedures for clearly defining the skill. Setting up a short counter-example where the skill is obviously missing is one way to emphasize the skill and illustrate the need for it at the same time.

Teachers should not try to teach too many skills at the same time. Start with one or two. One 1st-grade curriculum unit we have helped with teaches eight skills over a year's time, starting with "Everyone does a job" and including "Sharing ideas and materials," "Giving directions without being bossy," and "Caring about others' feelings."

Step 3. Set Up Practice Situations

To master a skill, students need to practice it again and again. The first practice session should be long enough for the skill to be fairly well learned by each student, and then short practice sessions should be distributed across several days or weeks. As students practice, teachers should continue to give verbal instructions and encourage students to perform the skills with proper sequence and timing. Some of the strategies found effective for encouraging practice are:

1. Assign specific roles to group members to ensure practice of the skills. A teacher, for example, could assign the roles of *reader, encourager, summarizer,* and *elaboration-seeker* to the members of a cooperative learning group. The roles could be rotated daily until every student has been responsible for each role several times.

2. Announce that the occurrence of the skills will be observed. It is surprising how much practice of a skill occurs when the teacher announces that he or she will be looking for a specific skill and stands next to a group with an observation sheet. The teacher's presence and the knowledge that the frequency of the skills is being counted and valued by the teacher (or a student observer) is a potent motivator of practice.

3. At times, a nonacademic group exercise may be given to provide students with a chance to practice cooperative skills. There may be times when an exercise that is fun and not part of the ongoing work of the class can be used to encourage students to practice specific skills. There are many such exercises available (Chasnoff, 1979; Johnson, 1981; Johnson and F. Johnson, 1982; Lyons, 1980; Roy, 1982).

New skills need to be cued consistently and reinforced for some time. Teachers should be relentless in encouraging prolonged use of cooperative skills.

Step 4. Ensure that Students Process Their Use of the Skills

Practicing cooperative skills is not enough. Students also need to discuss, describe, and reflect on their use of the skills in order to improve their performance. Processing how well students are using cooperative skills involves discussing how frequently and how effectively each student used the skills. To ensure that students discuss and give each other feedback about their use of the skills, teachers will have to provide time and set up procedures for processing. The following strategies may help:

1. Provide a regular time for processing. Ten minutes at the end of each period, or 20 minutes once a week, are typical.

2. Provide a set of procedures for students to follow. A processing sheet that the group fills out together, signs, and then hands in may be useful. Questions might include, "How many members felt they had a chance to share their ideas in their group?" and "How many members felt listened to?" The most effective procedure, however, is to have one member of the group observe the frequency with which each member engages in one of the targeted cooperative skills and, in the discussion at the end of the period, give each member feedback about their performance.

3. Provide opportunities for positive feedback among group members. One procedure is to have each member told by every other member one action that reflected effective use of a cooperative skill.

Teachers may have to model the processing initially and periodically so that students will take the processing seriously and become adept at doing it.

Step 5. Ensure that Students Persevere in Practicing the Skills

With most skills there is (1) a period of slow learning, (2) a period of rapid improvement, (3) a period where performance remains about the same, (4) another period of rapid improvement, (5) another plateau, and so forth. Students have to practice cooperative skills long enough to make it through the first few plateaus and integrate the skills into their behavioral repertoires. Most skill development goes through the following set of stages:

1. Awareness that the skill is needed.
2. Understanding of what the skill is.
3. Self-conscious, awkward engagement in the skill. Practicing any new skill feels awkward. The first few times someone throws a football, plays a piano, or paraphrases, it feels strange.
4. Feelings of phoniness while engaging in the skill. After a while the awkwardness passes and skill enactment becomes more smooth. Many students, however, feel that the skill is inauthentic or phony. Teacher and peer encouragement are needed to move the students through this stage.
5. Skilled but mechanical use of the skill.
6. Automatic, routine use where the skill is fully integrated into students' behavior repertoires and seems like a natural action to engage in.

In order for students to move from awareness to the automatic use of the skills, teachers have to encourage sustained practice of the skills over a long period of time. The goal for all collaborative skill learning is to reach the stage where teachers can structure a lesson cooperatively and have students automatically and naturally engage in a high level of collaborative skills while achieving their learning goals. Student and teacher rewards for reaching such a stage go far beyond increased achievement.

Conclusion

Nothing we learn is more important than the skills of collaboration. Most human interaction is cooperative. Without some skill in cooperating effectively, it would be difficult (if not impossible) to maintain a marriage, hold a job, or be part of a community, society, and world. In this chapter we have discussed only a few of the skills needed for effective cooperation. For a more thorough and extensive coverage of these skills, see *Reaching Out* (Johnson, 1981), *Joining Together* (Johnson and F. Johnson, 1982), *Human Relations and Your Career* (Johnson, 1978), and *Learning Together and Alone* (Johnson and Johnson, 1975).

5

Supervising Teachers' Use of Cooperative Learning

Teachers will not become proficient in using cooperative learning procedures by attending a workshop or from reading this book. Teachers become proficient and competent from *doing*. To develop the expertise in cooperative learning procedures teachers need to routinely structure a cooperative lesson without conscious planning or thought. They must use cooperative learning procedures regularly for several years and be given in-classroom help and assistance. This requires a supervisor, principal, or master teacher actively promoting the sustained use of cooperative learning procedures and setting up a professional support system to provide continuous, immediate, in-class assistance in perfecting teachers' competencies. To do this, supervisors and principals must:

1. Recognize the basic principles of mastering a new instructional strategy
2. Be able to differentiate effective from ineffective implementation (see Chapter 3)
3. Give up the individualistic perspective on supervising
4. Understand the purposes of professional support groups
5. Know how to structure and manage a professional support system.

Basic Principles of Mastering New Instructional Strategies

Although supervisors of teachers are probably versed in the basic principles of implementing new instructional strategies, we'd like to review the ones that we, and others, have found most effective in helping teachers learn to use cooperative learning (Berman and McLaughlin, 1978; Johnson, 1970, 1979; Lawrence, 1974; Little, 1981; McLaughlin and Marsh, 1978).

1. For the most part, teachers participating in the training are those who teach each other how to use cooperative learning procedures and who sustain each other's interest in doing so, not the consultants or individuals leading the training. This means that in order to implement cooperative learning procedures successfully, a professional support or growth system must be established among participating teachers.

2. Teachers must clearly understand what cooperative learning is and be given concrete strategies and specific skills on how to implement it in their classrooms. But effective training also means flexibility— allowing teachers to adapt cooperative learning to their own subject areas, curriculum materials, circumstances, and students. If teachers do the work to make the strategies their own, they will see cooperative learning as something they *want* to do, rather than something they are asked or required to do. Prepackaged, specific procedures that teachers have to use in preset ways are not a good idea, as they tend to be used for a while and then discontinued.

3. Effective training programs must be "hands on," and an integral part of the job, with help and support on-call when teachers need it. Such training would emphasize demonstrations, "hands on" trying out the strategies, and feedback. In addition, ongoing training over several years would be provided when individual teachers want and need it. Experts who can provide support and assistance should be on-call to demonstrate, co-teach, problem-solve, and to provide help when it is needed and wanted.

4. For implementation to be successful, teachers need support and advocacy from building and district administrators. Administrators must understand what cooperative learning strategies are and be able to recognize them in teachers' classrooms. In addition to supporting teachers who are struggling to master cooperative learning strategies, administrators should structure teacher-teacher work and cooperative relationships to demonstrate their support for the use of such strategies in the classroom.

5. In order for teachers to implement cooperative learning procedures on a routine level (where they can automatically structure a lesson cooperatively without preplanning or conscious thought), they need time to gain experience in an incremental step-by-step manner. Adoption of a new teaching practice requires substantial shifts in habits and routines. These shifts take time and should happen by degrees. Teachers should not be expected to become immediate experts on cooperative learning or else they will feel overwhelmed and unable to cope. When teachers are expected to gain expertise in too short a period of time, work overload and feelings of helplessness may result. Given enough time, teachers will experience increased confidence in their professional competence. Two years is the average amount of time required to become a skilled user of cooperative learning procedures.

Giving Up the Individualistic Perspective

Just as teachers in an individualistic program can become terribly overworked, so can superiors who have their work structured individualistically. It is not possible for a supervisor or principal to provide teachers with all the support, encouragement, feedback, and ongoing assistance they need to learn how to use cooperative learning procedures successfully. The individualistic perspective, where supervisors and principals are supposed to work with all teachers one-on-one, is not realistic when one examines how much support and assistance is necessary and how many other responsibilities principals and supervisors have. Such daily assistance need not be given personally. From this perspective, it makes sense to think in terms of professional support groups and structured cooperative interdependence rather than direct individual assistance and support and individual incentives for individual teachers. Behavior modification for teachers does not work. Supervisors and principals need to structure and manage the support system. They need not try to *be* the support system! Let the cooperative support system work for you and your district.

Professional Support Groups

While there are a number of people who have as part of their job description the supporting and assisting of teachers, not all are seen by teachers as equally helpful. Close supervision by principals has been frequently found to hurt the morale of teachers. When teachers are asked to identify their primary source of innovative ideas about teaching and their primary source of support and assistance, their response is usually "other teachers." Supervisors and principals who wish to establish effective professional support and assistance for teachers, therefore, turn to other teachers.

For effective implementation of cooperative learning procedures within a school or a school district, therefore, we suggest that you concentrate your efforts on structuring and managing professional teacher support groups within each school building. Professional support groups are safe places where:

1. Members like to be.
2. There is support, caring, concern, laughter, and camaraderie.
3. The primary goal of improving each other's competence in using cooperative learning procedures is never obscured.

Successfully implementing cooperative learning in schools depends on creating such a support and assistance system among the teachers being trained. Teachers will not only teach each other how to use cooperative learning procedures but also sustain each other's interest in doing so. Our best advice for long-term implementation of cooperative learning procedures is the formation of a professional support and assistance system among participating teachers.

The purpose of this professional support group is to work jointly and continuously to:

1. Help each other continue to gain competence in using cooperative learning procedures.
2. Serve as an informal support group for sharing, letting off steam, and discussing problems connected with implementing cooperative learning procedures.
3. Serve a base for teachers experienced in the use of cooperative learning procedures to teach other teachers how to structure and manage lessons cooperatively.
4. Provide camaraderie and shared success.

There is no doubt that teachers teach better when they experience support from their peers. In most schools, however, such support is hard to achieve. As a result, many teachers feel harried, isolated, and alienated. Yet there is a deep human need to work collaboratively and intimately with supportive people. Professional support group meetings provide teachers with the opportunity to share ideas, support each other's efforts to use cooperative learning procedures effectively, and encourage each other. If they meet on a regular basis to look more realistically and objectively at their implementation efforts, the result will be close, personal, collaborative relationships among members.

We have found that support groups succeed if they have clear goal interdependence, clear procedures, and active participation by members. Procedures must be clear-cut to avoid the degeneration of the meetings either into gripe sessions with destructive criticism of each other, or amateur therapy and sensitivity training at the other end of the spectrum. Task-oriented problem solving, as well as empathy and mutual support, should dominate the group's climate.

The three key activities of a professional support group are (Little, 1981):

1. Frequent professional discussions of cooperative learning, including sharing successes.
2. Co-planning, designing, preparing, and evaluating curriculum materials to implement cooperative learning in the classrooms of members.
3. Reciprocal observations of each other teaching a cooperatively structured lesson, and joint processing of those observations.

Each will be discussed in the following sections.

Professional Discussions

Within professional support groups there must be frequent, continuous, increasingly concrete and precise talk about the use of cooperative learning procedures. Through such discussion members build a concrete, precise, and coherent shared language, which can describe the complexity of using cooperative learning procedures, distinguish one practice and its virtues from another, and integrate cooperative learning procedures into other teaching practices and strategies already in use. In such discussions, teachers exchange successful procedures and materials. They focus on solving specific problems members may be having in perfecting their use of cooperative learning strategies.

Joint Planning and Curriculum Design

Members of professional support groups should frequently plan, design, prepare, and evaluate curriculum materials together. Teachers share the burden of developing materials needed to conduct cooperative lessons; generate emerging understanding of cooperative learning strategies; make realistic standards for students and colleagues; and provide the machinery for each other to implement cooperative learning procedures. The process of jointly planning a lesson with each conducting it and then processing it afterward, is often constructive.

Reciprocal Observations

Members of professional support groups should frequently observe each other teaching lessons structured cooperatively and then provide each other with useful feedback. Observation and feedback provide members with shared experiences; but to be beneficial the processes must be reciprocal. Teachers particularly need to show each other that they recognize that anyone can have good and bad days and that the mistakes they note in a colleague may be the same mistakes that they will make tomorrow.

We have found a number of important guidelines for teachers to follow when observing the teaching of other members of their professional support group. Teachers should:

1. Realize that they can learn from every member of the group, regardless of their experience and personal characteristics.
2. Ensure that observation and feedback are reciprocal.
3. Ask the person they're observing what he or she would like to have attention focused on. This may include specific students the teacher may wish observed, specific aspects of structuring interdependence or accountability, or another aspect of cooperative learning.
4. Focus feedback and comments on what has taken place, not on personal competence.
5. Not confuse a teacher's personal worth with his or her current level of competence in using cooperative learning procedures.
6. Be concrete and practical in their discussions about how effectively members are using cooperative learning procedures.
7. Above all, communicate respect for each other's overall teaching competence.

Helpful Norms for Support Groups

A number of helpful norms will help professional support groups function effectively. These norms include:

1. I don't have to be perfect and neither do you!
2. It takes time to master cooperative learning procedures to a routine-use level.
3. I'm here to improve my competence in using cooperative learning procedures.

4. You can criticize my implementation of cooperative learning procedures without my taking it personally.
5. I am secure enough to give you feedback about your implementation
   of cooperative learning procedures.

Figure 1. Differences Between PSG's and Traditional Teaming.

Professional Support Groups	Traditional Teams
Clear positive goal inter- dependence is structured among teachers	Teachers are told to work together
All members share leadership responsibilities	A team leader is assigned
Teachers are trained to function skillfully in collaborative groups	No skill training is provided
High individual accountability	No individual accountability
High joint rewards and incentives	Individual rewards and incentives

Structuring Professional Support Groups

Steps that supervisors and principals need to go through in structuring
and managing professional support groups aimed at implementing
cooperative learning procedures in the classroom include the following:

1. Publicly announce your support for the use of cooperative learning
   procedures
2. Recruit and select teachers to participate in the groups
3. Review with them the nature of cooperative learning
4. Highlight the goal interdependence among members of a professional support group
5. Negotiate a contract among the members of the professional support groups, and a contract between the professional support
   groups and you, if appropriate
6. Structure the first few meetings of the professional support group
   until members are able to structure them by themselves
7. Provide the resources and incentives needed for the groups to
   function
8. Ensure that the professional support groups discuss how well they
   function and maintain good relationships among members

9. Build yourself *in* as a member not *out* as a consultant
10. Keep a long-term, developmental perspective and protect the professional support groups from other pressures.

Each step will be discussed in the following sections.

Announcing Your Support

Forming teacher professional support groups, aimed at improving competencies in using cooperative learning procedures, begins with the supervisor or principal announcing support for teachers using such strategies. This should take place on important occasions such as beginning staff meetings. Such announcements should be frequent, and cooperative learning should be described concretely in terms of life in school. Teachers who are using cooperative learning procedures should be visibly and publicly praised. The message supervisors and principals should be giving is, "We approve of cooperative learning procedures; therefore the staff should strive to do so." During the year, give updates on new research or describe new procedures to implement cooperative learning. Relate how cooperative learning agrees with district and school goals. Tolerate and absorb any initial failures of teachers in learning how to structure lessons cooperatively. It is important that supervisors or principals do not kill cooperative learning by skepticism or neglect.

Recruiting Teachers

Teachers who are open, sensitive, supportive, and professionally competent will make good group members. Disgruntled, unconstructive teachers tend to ruin professional support groups. Their criticism is rarely productive, and they often lack wisdom in choosing battlegrounds. Alienated teachers may also be disruptive and demoralizing. And incompetent teachers who are struggling to survive are unprepared to begin professional growth until they gain basic control and self-confidence. Also, teachers who talk a different game than the one they play should be avoided. In other words, members should be handpicked to ensure the group's success. Helpful methods of recruiting and selecting members include:

1. Listening to and participating in teachers' conversations to find out who might be interested in perfecting their skills by using cooperative learning procedures
2. Bringing together teachers who like using cooperative learning procedures

3. Recruiting grade-level groups that already informally or formally serve as professional support groups
4. Recruiting teachers who are good friends with each other and who will welcome the opportunity to work more closely with each other
5. Recruiting teachers who have the same preparation period.

Reviewing the Nature of Cooperative Learning

After establishing the membership of a professional support group, it is helpful to review the nature of cooperative learning for all the members. The principal or supervisor may:

1. Recommend a training course or workshop in which they can participate
2. Arrange for them to observe a teacher who is highly experienced in using cooperative learning procedures
3. Provide reading material on cooperative learning
4. Have consultants or experienced teachers present an awareness session for all the school staff
5. Have the group meet with a district specialist in cooperative learning.

Highlighting Goal Interdependence

The basic goal of a professional support group is to work jointly and continuously to teach each other how to better use cooperative learning strategies. As with students working and learning collaboratively, members of professional support groups need to be made aware of the critical importance of their interdependence.

Negotiating Contracts

When teachers become part of a professional support group, they accept certain mutual responsibilities. These include a willingness to:

1. Attend the meetings of the professional support group
2. Commit themselves to increasing their competence in using cooperative learning procedures
3. Commit themselves to helping other members increase their competence in using cooperative learning procedures
4. Discuss their use of cooperative learning procedures and engage in problem solving to improve the implementation efforts of themselves and other members

5. Share the task of incorporating cooperative learning into existing curriculum materials with the other members of the group
6. Ask other members to observe periodically as they teach cooperatively structured lessons and to provide them with feedback
7. Agree to observe the other members teach cooperatively structured lessons and to provide them with feedback
8. Contribute constructively to the goal achievement of the professional support group and to the maintenance of high-quality working relationships among members.

These responsibilities need to be put into a formally agreed-upon contract so that there is a basis for discussing how well the professional support group is functioning. The responsibilities of supervisors and principals in structuring and managing the professional support group need to be clear in order to legitimize their involvement in the group. For instance, the group is not a place for supervisors to evaluate individual teachers, and group members should be aware that such is not the intent.

Structuring the Initial Meetings

The activities of the professional support group are aimed at helping all members master, refine, adapt, and experiment with cooperative learning procedures. Discussing their implementation efforts, jointly planning lessons and jointly designing curriculum materials, and reciprocally observing each other's implementation efforts are the major activities of the group.

At the first meeting of the professional support group, we recommend that the supervisor or principal:

1. Express support of the group's efforts in implementing cooperative learning procedures.
2. Agree on a regular meeting time. (The meeting must last at least 50 to 60 minutes.)
3. Review the purposes of these meetings (discussion of implementation efforts, joint planning of lessons and materials, and reciprocal observation).
4. Ask what resources members need in order to meet regularly and engage in these activities. (Potential resources are discussed in the next section.)
5. Design the meeting to be both productive and fun. With that in mind, the principal or supervisor might ask who is going to be in

charge of the refreshments for the next meeting. (A cooperative effort is recommended.)

6. Specifically have *the group members* plan:
   a. When the next meeting will be
   b. What cooperatively structured lessons they will teach before the next meeting
   c. What the agenda for the next meeting will be, such as discussing how well their cooperatively structured lessons went.
7. Agree on tentative contracts: among group members and between the group and the principal or supervisor.

A sample agenda for the second meeting is for the principal or supervisor to:

1. Welcome everyone and have a "warm-up," such as a handout on the types of positive interdependence that may be used in cooperatively structured lessons
2. Discuss their use of cooperative learning procedures:
   a. Lessons taught during the past week
   b. Their successes—what were the things they liked best
   c. Any problems that surfaced during the lessons
3. Discuss the problems at some length and generate alternative strategies for solving each, so that each member may select from a menu of alternative solutions rather than having to implement any one solution
4. Jointly plan a lesson that will be taught by all members during the following week
5. Plan the agenda and menu for the next meeting.

At the third meeting the principal or supervisor may:

1. Warm up by handing out a list of ways to ensure individual accountability in cooperatively structured lessons
2. Discuss how well the lesson they taught went, identifying positive aspects and problems that arose
3. Discuss the problems, generate possible solutions, and revise the lesson to solve any problems
4. Plan for as many of the members as possible to observe each other teach a lesson structured cooperatively during the following week; make specific contracts as to what the observer should focus on; perhaps make an outline of the teacher's role in cooperative learning situations
5. Set agenda and menu for the following week.

At the fourth meeting, the principal or supervisor may wish to:

1. Warm up by handing out material on teaching students the social skills on which they need to work collaboratively
2. Discuss how well the observations went and what the members observed; review the roles for constructive feedback (see Johnson, 1981); review the basic components of cooperative learning situations; and ensure that all feedback is constructive and helpful
3. Plan for the next round of observations
4. Set the agenda and the menu for the next meeting.

These sample agendas are only aimed at outlining what might happen in the initial meetings of the professional support groups. Agendas will need to be revised to best meet the needs of specific teachers.

Providing Resources and Incentives

Teachers' perceptions of their interdependence may be considerably enhanced if principals or supervisors offer joint incentives for effective professional support groups. Incentives can be classified as tangible, interpersonal, and personal. Some examples of incentives we have found valuable are:

1. The opportunity to present an inservice session on cooperative learning procedures to other members of the staff or to the staff of another school
2. The opportunity to apply for summer salaries to revise curriculum for cooperatively structured lessons
3. Visible public praise for teachers' efforts in implementing cooperative learning procedures
4. Written recognition of their efforts to go into their individual files
5. The opportunity to observe teachers in other schools implementing cooperative learning procedures.

The more tangible incentives supervisors and principals can offer professional support groups as a whole, the greater the perceived interdependence may be among teachers. A maxim developed within the business/industrial sector of our society states, "If two individuals get paid for working as a pair, it is amazing how much interest they take in helping one another succeed!"

To be effective, a professional support group needs a variety of resources that only supervisors and principals can provide. Needed resources include:

1. Released time during working hours to meet

2. A small fund for materials and expenses to implement cooperative learning
3. Released time to observe each other teach cooperative lessons
4. Released time to visit the classrooms of teachers in other schools who are experienced in using cooperative learning procedures
5. Materials on cooperative learning, such as research updates, helpful hints, sample lesson plans, books, and so forth
6. Supervisory time and resources to help them get started and to help them maintain high interest and involvement in implementing cooperative learning procedures in their classrooms
7. Emotional support and encouragement from principal or supervisor to continue their efforts.

Always remember that pressure (however subtle) on teachers to implement cooperative learning procedures in their classrooms must be coupled with tangible and visible support from the principal or supervisor.

Discussing How Well the Professional Support Groups Function

One area in which most teacher professional support groups need considerable help and encouragement is in discussing how well their meetings are contributing to achieving the group's goals and to maintaining effective working relationships among members. This means that the principal or supervisor will need to take some initiative in ensuring that one teacher periodically and systematically observes a meeting and that time is spent in processing how well the group is functioning. After the teachers become experienced in helping their student groups discuss their group functioning, the teachers' abilities to discuss the functioning of their own meetings should increase. But even the most experienced teachers may avoid discussing the functioning of meetings unless the supervisors or principals structure it.

Building Yourself in As a Member

As principal or supervisor, you should be part of each professional support group in your jurisdiction. Build yourself in, not out! Do not be lonely! Members of a professional support group will enjoy considerable success, feel a sense of accomplishment, like each other, see each other as supportive and accepting, and have a sense of camaraderie that significantly increases the quality of their professional lives. You should be part of these feelings!

Protecting and Nuturing

When teachers become serious about implementing cooperative learning procedures in their classrooms, supervisors and principals will have to do a number of things to protect and nurture their efforts. Some examples follow.

1. There will inevitably be initial failures and problems. Students may be unhappy about the change in the "system"; students will be unskilled in working collaboratively; materials may be inappropriate; teacher and supervisors may have different definitions of cooperative learning. Allowances will have to be made for these initial problems. Such initial "start-up costs" are to be expected and accepted. Teachers cannot be expected to be perfect during the first week they try structuring lessons cooperatively!

2. There will be other innovations within a supervisor's jurisdiction that will compete for teachers' attention and energy. Part of a supervisor's responsibility is to find commonalities of interest and intent among presumably opposing innovations. Teachers should be encouraged to integrate cooperative learning with other instructional strategies they already use or are trying out. The cycle of making cooperative learning the focus for a few months or a year and then springing another innovation on teachers should be avoided at all costs. The "try it and then drop it for the next fad" cycle is especially destructive to quality teaching. Teacher and supervisor commitment to cooperative learning has to span a number of years.

3. The meaning of cooperative learning should be translated so that diverse groups of teachers can understand its importance and usefulness.

4. Supervisors should deflect, soften, and negate resistance to implementing cooperative learning within their staffs. If some teachers believe "I tried that once and it did not work," supervisors should protect the teachers who *are* willing to become involved in implementing cooperative learning in their classrooms from demoralizing conversations and criticism from such colleagues.

5. Within any staff there may be destructive competition among teachers as to who is best. Supervisors should defuse such "win-lose" dynamics and encourage mutual respect, support, and assistance among all teachers.

6. Within any professional support group there will come a time when one member has hurt the feelings of another member or when conflicts arise that disrupt the cohesiveness and productivity of the

group. At that point the supervisor's task is to ensure that hurt feelings become repaired and that conflicts are constructively resolved.

7. Most teachers are concerned about whether or not they will receive strong support from their principal and supervisors if a parent complains about their use of cooperative learning procedures. If parents are concerned and involved in their children's education, they may be curious or even skeptical at any modification of teaching procedures. Supervisors must be ready to justify why a teacher is using cooperative learning procedures and to give full support and approval.

8. Supervisors must have the courage to see their teachers through the process of learning how to use cooperative learning procedures effectively.

Thinking Developmentally

It takes time to master cooperative learning procedures so that they are used routinely. For most teachers, proficiency does not come in a few weeks or even in a few months. Supervisors should always think in terms of development, not in radically changing everything the teacher is doing immediately. After teachers perfect their procedures in one area, they can then expand to a second area. The focus should be on developmental planning for a two- or three-year process with heavy emphasis on supporting and maintaining interest.

Diane Browne's Strategy

An outstanding implementer of cooperative learning procedures within a school district is Diane Browne of the Hopkins School District in Minnesota. Her primary responsibility is to supervise and support teachers within the district in their implementation of cooperative learning procedures. General procedures that Browne has used in institutionalizing cooperative learning within her school district are as follows:

1. She gives a general awareness inservice session to an entire school and asks for volunteers to become a school-based professional support group, which will work systematically on improving teachers' skills in using cooperative learning procedures.

2. Browne then works with each teacher individually: she first teaches a cooperatively structured lesson in the classroom; she then sits

down with the teacher and co-plans a cooperatively structured lesson, which they will jointly teach; they then co-plan a lesson for the
teacher to teach while Browne observes. Through repeated classroom visits Browne trains each teacher one-on-one. Some of her
basic rules for working with an individual teacher are:
   a. All lessons are prepared together.
   b. The teacher is the expert on his or her classroom, and Browne is
      the expert on cooperative learning.
   c. When she is in the classroom, the teacher owns the lesson. It is
      the teacher's lesson, not Browne's.
3. Each time Browne meets with a teacher, she offers a new helpful
   technique or set of materials, which is tailored to the teacher's
   subject area or to a specific problem student in the teacher's classroom. This adds a personal as well as a professional aspect to the
   help and assistance in implementing cooperative learning procedures.
4. After a number of teachers are trained within a school, they begin
   meeting as a professional support group with and without Browne.
5. As an additional maintenance procedure, Browne sends out a
   monthly newsletter on "How to Help Students Work in Groups."
   These newsletters contain lesson plans and classroom activities that
   teachers can try out and/or discuss in the support group meetings.
6. Besides meeting with the professional support groups, Browne regularly meets with curriculum directors, talks to parent groups, at-
   tends the principals' cabinet meetings, trouble-shoots for her
   teachers, coordinates collaboration between regular classroom and
   special education teachers, and generally spends her days in schools
   and classrooms.
7. Browne's success can be attributed to her genuine enthusiasm about
   the use of cooperative learning procedures, her ability to build
   personal and supportive relationships with practically all the
   teachers she works with, her ingenuity in discovering ways to help
   teachers using cooperative learning procedures, and the willingness
   of her school district to fund her position as a teacher facilitator.

Not all districts are lucky enough to have a person like Diane Browne on
their staff, and not all districts are farsighted enough to place such tal-
ented people in positions where they can work one-on-one with teachers
interested in implementing cooperative learning procedures. But with
luck or foresight, any district can find itself supporting cooperative learning.

On Teacher Morale

Most educators agree that teaching is not as much fun as it used to be. Many schools lack supportiveness and collegiality. Teaching has become a lonely profession. A feeling of isolation from their peers is a major contributing factor to the low morale and lack of continuing professional growth generally found among teachers. And the profession hardly commands the respect it once had.

A number of studies conclude that teachers are less satisfied with the quality of their work lives and are more likely to experience problems with their jobs than most Americans. There is also evidence that teachers tend to gain competence for approximately their first three years of teaching, maintain a plateau for about 20 years, and then gradually decline in competence.

Structuring teachers into professional support groups can have important effects on teacher morale as well as on their competence in using cooperative learning procedures. Developing a clear cooperative interdependence among teachers has many advantages over encouraging competitive or individualistic relationships. There is a deep human need to collaborate and build personal relationships with supportive peers; it may be just as important among teachers as it is among students. And not only do teachers need to learn how to use cooperative learning procedures with students, but principals and other administrators may need to learn how to structure cooperative relationships among teachers.

6

Myths About Cooperative Learning

Among the questions repeatedly asked by teachers and administrators during training sessions on cooperative learning, some come from untrue assumptions about how school ought to be and what students should be trained to do. This chapter discusses a series of such questions based on false assumptions and explores a few myths about schools and teaching.

Myth 1: Schools Should Emphasize Competition Because It's a Dog-Eat-Dog World

Not true. It is a person-help-person world. When you look closely, you will find that almost all human activity is cooperative. We work in an economic system characterized by an elaborate division of labor, and we live in families and communities held together by our common interests. Like all social systems, our educational system is based on coordinating the actions of many individuals to achieve mutual goals. We live in an interdependent world. It goes on and on. Giraffes have survived as a species because of their long necks, cheetahs because of their speed, and humans because of our ability to cooperate to achieve mutual goals. Cooperation is such an integral part of human existence that, like a fish trying to be aware of water, we only know it's there when it breaks down.

To make school life more realistic, classrooms should be dominated by cooperative learning activities. This does not, however, mean that students should not learn how to compete appropriately for fun and enjoyment, win or lose. When the overall context is cooperative, competition provides an interesting and enjoyable change of pace without students believing that winning is a life or death matter. We also believe that some individualistic work, where students work autonomously and take responsibility to follow through on a task, is essential. Cooperatively structured lessons should prepare students both to do similar work alone and to provide a setting in which individual accomplishments and competencies are used to contribute to the overall achievement of the group. We would be very disappointed to see *only* cooperative learning being used within a classroom, but we are pragmatic enough to recognize that cooperation is the key to an effective classroom learning climate.

Myth 2: High-Achieving Students Are Penalized by Working in Heterogeneous Cooperative Learning Groups

To most educators, it is obvious that low- and middle-achieving students have much to gain by working in cooperative learning groups with high-achieving peers. In terms of both motivation and actual achievement, the largest gainers from working in heterogeneous cooperative learning groups are the struggling, low-achieving students; the next largest gainers are the middle-achievers.

What is not so obvious to many educators is that high-achieving students benefit in a number of ways from collaborating with low- and middle-achieving peers. We and others around the country have conducted numerous studies comparing the achievement of high-, middle-, and low-achieving students in cooperative, competitive, and individualistic learning situations. The high-achievers working in heterogeneous cooperative groups have never done worse than their counterparts working competitively or individualistically, and often they do better. When research investigates aspects of achievement other than test scores, the benefits for high-achieving students are more apparent. High-achieving students working in heterogeneous learning groups score higher on retention tests than do high-achievers who participate in competitive or individualistic learning situations. The quality of reasoning strategies used by the high-achievers was higher when they were in cooperative learning situations. The cognitive processes involved in having to talk through and explain (perhaps in several different ways) the material being studied seem to enhance retention and promote the development of higher-level reasoning strategies. It may be that bright students get quick, intuitive, correct answers to problems, but they may not have a conscious strategy for getting the answer. There is growing evidence that a silent student is a student who is not engaging in all of the cognitive processes necessary for high-quality learning.

An equally important benefit for high-achievers participating in heterogeneous cooperative learning groups is the development of collaborative skills and the friendships that can result. While bright students are often resented and sometimes ostracized in a competitive setting, they are seen as desirable partners in a cooperative setting. And in collaborating with middle- and low-achieving peers (as well as other bright students), high-achievers are more likely to develop the leadership, communication, decision making, and conflict management skills needed for future career success.

Myth 3: Every Member of a Cooperative Learning Group Has to Do the Same Work and Proceed at the Same Rate

When mainstreaming academically handicapped students into the regular classroom, many educators believe that cooperative learning procedures are not possible because the handicapped students cannot do work on the same level and at the same speed as the other students in the class. Such may be the case, but there are important advantages for having handicapped students collaborating with nonhandicapped peers and vice versa. The impact on collaborative skills, friendships, appreciation of human diversity, perspective-taking ability, and quality of life is considerable. And ways can be found to surmount the various learning capabilities of group members.

Each student in a cooperative learning group can be given different material to learn. In a spelling group, for example, each student can have a different set of words and/or a different number of words to learn. In a math class, each group member can have a different set of problems and/or a different number of problems to solve. Academically handicapped students may be evaluated according to different criteria so that the other group members are not penalized. Members of the same learning group can discuss, edit, check, and correct each other's work without working on the same material or at the same speed.

Myth 4: A Single Group Grade Shared by Group Members Is Not Fair

Having students work together on a joint product is viewed by many educators as being less fair to each student than is having each student work alone to produce an individual product for which he or she receives an individual grade. Most students would disagree. It is important that students perceive the distribution of grades and other rewards as being fair, otherwise they may become unmotivated and withdraw psychologically or physically. There have been several investigations of students' views of the fairness of various grading systems. There are five major findings:

1. Students who "lose" in a competitive learning situation commonly perceive the grading system as being unjust and, consequently, dislike the class and the teacher (Johnson and Johnson, 1975).
2. Before a task is performed, students generally perceive a competitive grading system as being the most fair, but after a task is completed, having all members receive the same grade or reward is viewed as the fairest (Deutsch, 1979).
3. The more frequently students have experienced long-term cooperative learning experiences, and the more cooperative learning was used in their classes, then the more the students believed that everyone who tries has an equal chance to succeed in class, that students get the grades they deserve, and that the grading system is fair (Johnson and Johnson, 1983).
4. Students who have experienced cooperative learning prefer group grades over individual ones (Wheeler and Ryan, 1973).
5. Achievement is higher when group grades (compared with individual ones) are given (Johnson and Johnson, 1975).

The implications of this research for teachers is that group grades may be perceived to be unfair by students *before* the students have participated in a cooperative learning activity. Once cooperation has been experienced for a while, however, a single group grade will probably be perceived as the fairest method of evaluation.

There are three general systems for distributing rewards within our society: *equity* (the person who contributes the most or scores the highest receives the greatest reward), *equality* (every participant receives the same reward), and *need* (those who have the greatest need receive the greatest reward) (Deutsch, 1975). All three systems operate within our society, and all three systems have ethical rationales. Typically, the equality system assures members of a family, community, organization, or society that their basic needs will be met and that diverse contributions will be equally valued. The need system assures members that in moments of crisis others will provide support and assistance. And the equity system assures members that if they strive for excellence, their contributions will be valued and rewarded. Educators who wish to give rewards in the classroom merely on the basis of equity may be viewing "fairness" from too limited a perspective.

In the ideal classroom, at the end of a grading period, each student will have a number of grades resulting from collaborative efforts, a number of grades resulting from individualistic efforts, and a number of grades resulting from competitive efforts. When these grades are added together by teachers we have worked with, they inevitably, find that high-achievers get A's. Because of the higher achievement found in cooperative learning situations, however, middle- and low-achievers may receive higher grades than they would if the classroom was dominated by competitive or individualistic learning situations. The number of students receiving B's and C's will tend to grow larger as the positive peer pressure and support raises achievement. The number of D's and F's will tend to disappear as collaborators refuse to allow unmotivated students to stay that way. In order not to undermine the overall class collaborativeness, it is important to use a criterion-referenced evaluation system in determining final grades.

For teachers who want to give individual grades *within* cooperative learning situations, there are a number of alternatives that have been successfully used:

1. Bonus-point method: Students work together in cooperative learning groups, prepare each other for the test, take the test individually, and receive an individual grade. If all members of their group, however, achieve up to a preset criterion of excellence, then each member is rewarded bonus points.
2. Dual-grading system: Students work together in cooperative learning groups, prepare each other for the test, take the test individually, and receive an individual grade. They then receive a second grade based on the total performance of all group members.
3. Alternative reward: Same as "2" except that the group grade is used to determine whether group members receive a nonacademic reward, such as free time, extra recess time, or popcorn.

A science teacher in Austin, Texas, uses a grading system we like. Students work in cooperative learning groups during the week. The students take a weekly examination individually and that score becomes their base score. They then receive five bonus points if all group members

score above 60 percent on the test. This encourages intergroup cooperation. The teacher's latest addition to the system is to give another five
bonus point to every student if all students in the five science classes score
above 60 percent on the test. This encourages cooperation across classes.
We have a mental image of students going through the hall asking others,
"Are you taking science? Take your book home and study!"

Myth 5: Cooperative Learning Is Simple

Wrong! Cooperative learning helps increase the quality of life within
the classroom, students' achievement and critical thinking ability, and
students' long-term well-being and success. But it is not easy to implement. The concept of cooperation is simple. But switching a classroom
from an emphasis on individualistic and competitive learning to a classroom dominated by collaboration is a complex and long-term process.

Learning how to structure learning situations cooperatively is much
like peeling an onion. The teacher learns how to structure productive
cooperative learning activities layer by layer until the heart is reached.
Over a period of years of cooperation, the learning experiences become
richer and richer. The "layers" might include: learning how to place
students in productive groups and structuring cooperative learning goals;
monitoring and intervening to improve students' collaborative skills;
directly teaching students cooperative skills; experimenting with various
ways of arranging curriculum materials to promote positive interdependence; promoting academic controversies within the cooperative learning
groups; and finally, the integration of cooperative learning activities with
competitive and individualistic learning activities. There is nothing simple in such a process. But the results are worth it.

Myth 6: Schools Can Change Overnight

Wrong again! Fads come and go quickly, but transforming classrooms
into places where students care about each other's learning and work
cooperatively takes time. Where cooperative learning is concerned, we
believe more in "evolution" than "revolution". How cooperative learning has been implemented has differed in school districts, but all successful implementations have evolved over a period of time and have had
ongoing support. Consider the following example.

The Jefferson County School District in Lakewood, Colorado, took a
teacher-oriented and multiple-entry approach to implementing cooperative learning. The teacher-oriented approach first provides teachers with

basic training and then responds administratively to teachers' requests for further training and support rather than imposing cooperative learning from the administrative level. The multiple-entry approach means that after teacher interest is established in the district, cooperative learning is implemented in a variety of ways. Because it is being introduced in so many areas, teachers perceive that using it is inevitable. The procedure Jefferson County used is as follows:

1. The district gave the basic introductory course on the systematic use of cooperative, competitive, and individualistic learning several times for any teachers who were interested in taking it. The result was a network of several hundred teachers scattered throughout the district who were interested in using cooperative learning procedures.

2. The introductory course was then given a number of times on a demand basis for entire school staffs or for teams of teachers from the same school. This began a process of having schools make cooperative learning a major focus of their staff development efforts.

3. An introductory mini-course for administrators was then given a number of times for interested principals and school district personnel. These sessions ensured that administrators understood the nature of cooperative learning and its value for the district.

4. A number of teachers and central office staff were intensively trained to teach the basic course within the district. This provided Jefferson County with a cadre of experts who could train their teachers in cooperative learning.

5. As Jefferson County writes much of its own curriculum, teachers experienced in using cooperative learning procedures were placed on curriculum writing teams. Cooperative learning procedures were then written into the 1st- and 2nd-grade social studies/science curriculums. These curriculums included a series of lessons specifically aimed at teaching 1st- and 2nd-grade students the collaborative skills they need to work effectively as part of cooperative learning groups. Cooperative learning procedures were also written into a junior high school science curriculum.

6. The mainstreaming program within the district began to focus on the use of cooperative learning procedures to integrate handicapped students into constructive and supportive relationships with nonhandicapped peers.

7. Many social workers and school psychologists in the district participated in a mini-course on the use of cooperative learning proce-

dures to build a "therapeutic milieu" within the regular classroom where emotionally disturbed students could build better social skills and more constructive relationships with their peers.

8. Cooperative learning procedures were presented within district inservice course as a major procedure for classroom management and for decreasing absenteeism.

9. Jefferson County identified a number of master teachers highly skilled in the use of cooperative learning procedures whose classrooms would be used as demonstration sites for teachers to see cooperative learning in action.

10. Jefferson County next used their own staff to conduct a series of district courses on cooperative learning. These courses included:

   a. An introductory course on the effective and systematic use of cooperative, competitive, and individualistic learning procedures.
   b. An advanced course on teaching collaborative skills to students as an integrated part of using cooperative learning procedures.
   c. An advanced course on adapting specific curriculum used by participating teachers for cooperative learning.
   d. A course for principals on how to support and supervise teachers using cooperative learning procedures.

11. Jefferson County formed a regional center in which surrounding school districts interested in implementing cooperative learning could use Jefferson County personnel for inservice sessions and basic courses for teachers on the effective use of cooperative learning procedures.

Through these procedures Jefferson County School District has established cooperative learning within their district as one of the basic teaching strategies for quality instruction. For information on classrooms and programs, please contact Jim Metzdorf and Cherie Lyons (*Staff Development*); Harold Pratt and B. J. Meadows (*Topics in Science*); Marge Melle (*Primary Integrated Curriculum*); and Cindy Hrebar, Sally Ogden, and Diane Bergeron (*Cooperative Training*).

Where to See Cooperative Learning Groups in Action

Given that:
1. It's a people-help-people world
2. All students, including high-achievers, benefit from participating in heterogeneous cooperative learning groups

3. Different assignments may be given to different members of a cooperative learning group when it is desirable to do so
4. When teachers wish to do so, group grades may be given and will be
   perceived as fair by most students
5. Cooperative learning procedures have a richness that takes a teacher
   several years to explore,

the next question is: where can an interested educator see cooperative
learning in action?

In the East

1. Simmons College in Boston has included training in cooperative
   learning in its M.A. Program in special education. Interested parties
   can contact faculty member Deborah Mesch.
2. Robert Chasnoff, a professor at Keane College in Union, New Jersey, has worked with a number of nearby school districts and has
   helped train college professors in the use of cooperative learning.
   South Brunswick School District in New Jersey has a number of
   elementary and secondary teachers who are skilled in using cooperative learning. Princeton, New Jersey, is one of the few school
   districts to have a cooperative learning resource person working in
   the district.
3. The University of Vermont has spearheaded work throughout their
   state. Ann Nevin is one of the best contacts for school districts to
   visit.

In the Midwest

1. In Michigan, the Macomb Intermediate District near Detroit is actively involved in implementing cooperative learning in their school
   districts. A team of trainers headed by Ralph Pritchard conducts a
   number of training and follow-up sessions throughout the year. At
   Kalamazoo, Pat Wilson O'Leary and Dee Dishon actively train
   teachers and have developed several sets of materials that will be
   helpful to interested educators.
2. In Wisconsin, the Madison, Beloit, and Janesville School Districts
   have classrooms to visit.
3. In Elgin, Illinois, Sue Ford has done extensive work on cooperative
   learning as a teacher and a teacher trainer, as a trainer of principals
   who want to support cooperative learning in their schools. She is
   now an elementary school principal in the district.

4. In Lincoln, Nebraska, there has been extensive training of teachers. The principal of Park School has actively supported the use of cooperative learning. Lincoln School District has a resource teacher available to provide in-classroom assistance to teachers. Contact Betty Dillon-Peterson.

5. The Cooperative Learning Center has a strong tie in the state of Louisiana. For information on programs and teachers, contact Virginia Lyons, Opelousas Foundation; Betty Cole, Department of Nursing, University of Southwest Louisiana; or Antoine Garibaldi, Xavier University of Louisiana.

In the West

1. Secondary science teachers in Austin, Texas, have been active users of cooperative learning for several years. Contact Wayne Shade.

2. Jefferson County School District in Colorado is one of the most active districts in the country in cooperative learning. They are now collaborating with Denver and other nearby districts in providing mutual support and assistance in implementing cooperative learning. One of many outstanding contacts in Jefferson County is James Metzdorf.

3. Work on ethnic desegregation of the schools in San Diego School District includes training in how to use ethnically heterogeneous cooperative learning groups.

4. Leadership training has been conducted with the California Special Education Resource Network, and active training programs on cooperative learning are going on in a number of school districts throughout the state, from Redlands to Santa Barbara to Sacramento. For information about training sessions and classrooms to visit, contact the Resource Service Center, 1150 Eastern Ave., Sacramento, CA 95825.

5. To observe a college professor using cooperative learning in college classes, contact Brenda Bryant at the University of California, Davis.

Around the World

1. Gayle Hughes in the Provincial Department of Cooperation in Saskatchewan, Canada, can provide teachers with visits throughout the province and in the universities in Regina and Saskatoon.

2. In Montreal, Albert Weiner has been working with the Baldwin-

Cartier District and is a good contact for work on cooperative learning being done there and in the Montreal area.

3. In Sweden, John Steinberg at Orebro College can provide information about work on cooperative learning being done in Sweden.
4. In Norway, Egil Hjertaker at the Teachers College in Bergen or Per Kvist, Director of Education of County Hordaland, can provide locations of teachers using cooperative learning procedures in Norway.
5. In Australia, Lee Owens, who teaches at the University of Sydney, can provide information about teachers using cooperative learning procedures in Australia.

Do Not Forget Us

The Cooperative Learning Center (202 Pattee Hall, University of Minnesota) is where we plan and conduct research studies, do our writing, make movies, and develop new procedures for improving cooperative learning in the classroom and school. Here interested parties will find David Johnson, Roger Johnson, and Pat Roy. Edythe Johnson Holubec can now be reached at the University of Texas in Austin.

Sagamore Institute in the Adirondacks is the site of our summer training and is the only site where leadership training in implementing cooperative learning regularly takes place.

There are numerous teachers and principals accomplished in using cooperative learning strategies in the Minneapolis/St. Paul metropolitan area. Many of them are experienced in demonstrating their use of cooperative learning to interested visitors.

1. Webster School in St. Paul has been one of our research sites. Margaret Tiffany, a staff member from the Cooperative Learning Center, teaches there. It is a magnet inner-city elementary school.
2. Hopkins School District employs Diane Browne to provide continuous training and classroom follow-up in cooperative learning. Diane is currently involved in the use of cooperative learning procedures with computers. She is an expert on the use of cooperative learning to promote effective mainstreaming.
3. Moundsview School District is another site. Pike Lake School has integrated cooperative learning into the school program and has instituted an effective parent advocacy component through the efforts of Ron Sweeley. At the high school, Larry Gannon (who is featured in the movie, *Circles of Learning*) is using cooperative learning procedures in business classes.

Summary

Why is it that research so strongly supports cooperative learning and yet most classrooms are places where students work alone and where cooperation is discouraged? We don't know the full answer yet, but it is evident that there are strong forces that promote sameness in teaching. The barriers to transforming classrooms into cooperative places are real, and many myths about working alone are believed. This chapter has explored a few of the myths and listed a variety of places where teachers have conquered the barriers. Implementing cooperative learning is not easy and will not happen overnight, but the results are worth it.

7 Reflections

In the past many educators were given a choice of either working on one crisis or the other. Emphasis on reading and math was often placed in ways that increased student alienation and isolation. Emphasis on collaborative skills and friendships was often placed in ways that decreased student achievement. One of the major messages of this book is that *educators may have their cake and eat it too*. Cooperative learning allows educators to promote both higher achievement and healthy social and cognitive development simultaneously.

There is a long tradition of using cooperative learning strategies in U.S. education. Although cooperative learning has been ignored the past 50 years or so, it is now being rediscovered. Not only is there considerable research to validate the effectiveness of cooperative learning, but there are clear procedures for teachers to follow and a clear supervisory model available. The myths supporting the overuse and inappropriate use of individualistic and competitive learning are being disspelled. What now remains is for the mature teaching force within the United States to modify their teaching practices to bring them into line with what is known about effective instruction and constructive social and cognitive development.

This book has many key messages:

1. Cooperative, competitive, and individualistic learning are all important and should all be used, but the dominant goal structure in the class should be cooperation.

2. Whenever a learning task is assigned, a clear goal structure should be given so that students know what behaviors are appropriate within the lesson. The basic elements of the cooperative goal structure are positive interdependence, individual accountability, face-to-face interaction, and cooperative skills.

3. The teacher's role in structuring learning situations cooperatively involves clearly specifying the objectives for the lesson, placing students in productive learning groups and providing appropriate materials, clearly explaining the cooperative goal structure, monitoring students as they work, and evaluating students' performance. The students should always be aware that they "sink or swim together" in a cooperative learning situation.

4. For cooperative learning groups to be productive, students must be able to engage in the needed collaborative skills. Teaching cooperative skills can be done simultaneously with teaching academic material.

5. Given the mature teaching force within the United States, and given the demoralization found within many school staffs, the implementation of cooperative learning needs to be coupled with the implementation of collaborative professional support groups among educators. Both the success of implementation efforts and the quality of life within most schools depend on teachers and other staff members cooperating with each other. Support for the programs takes as careful structuring and monitoring as does cooperative learning.

6. There are a number of myths prevalent within U.S. schools that may impede the implementation of cooperative learning. When these myths become bothersome, contact the authors of this book or educators experienced in the use of cooperative learning for support.

References

Aronson, E.; Blaney, N.; Stephan, C.; Sikes, J.; and Snapp, M. *The Jigsaw Classroom.* Beverly Hills, Calif.: Sage Publictions, 1978.

Basic Skills in the U.S. Workforce. New York: Center for Public Resources, 1983.

Becker, G. *Human Capital.* Chicago: University of Chicago Press, 1975.

Belonging (motion picture). Edina, Minn.: Interaction Book Company, 1980.

Berman, P., and McLaughlin, M. *Federal Programs Supporting Educational Change, Vol. VIII: Implementing and Sustaining Innovations.* Santa Monica, Calif.: Rand Corpration, 1978.

Bronfenbrenner U. "Who Cares For America's Children?"In *The Family—Can It Be Saved?* Edited by V. Vaughan and T. Brazelton. New York: Year Book Medical Publishers, 1976.

Bybee, R., and Gee, E. *Violence, Values, and Justice in the Schools.* Boston: Allyn and Bacon, 1982.

Campbell, J. "The Children's Crusader: Colonel Francis W. Parker." Ph.D. dissertation, Teachers College, Columbia University, 1965.

Chasnoff, R., ed. *Structuring Cooperative Learning Experiences in the Classroom: The 1979 Handbook.* Edina, Minn.: Interaction Book Company, 1979.

Circles of Learning (motion picture). Edina, Minn.: Interaction Book Company, 1983.

Comber, L. C., and Keeves, John P. *Science Education in Nineteen Countries.* Stockholm and New York: Almquist & Wiksell and Wiley-Halstead, 1983.

Deutsch, M. "Cooperation and Trust: Some Theoretical Notes." In *Nebraska Symposium on Motivation.* Edited by M. R. Jones. Lincoln: University of Nebraska Press, 1962, pp. 275-319.

———— . "Equity, Equality, and Need. What Determines Which Values Will Be Used as the Basis of Distributive Justice?" *Journal of Social Issues* 31 (1975): 137-149.

———— . "A Critical Review of Equity Theory: An Alternative Perspective on the Social Psychology of Justice." *International Journal of Group Tensions* 9 (1979): 20-49.

DeVries, D., and Edwards K. "Learning Games and Student Teams: Their Effects on Classroom Process." *American Educational Research Journal* 10 (1973): 307-318.

Johnson, D. W. *The Social Psychology of Education.* New York: Holt, Rinehart & Winston, 1970.

———— . *Human Relations and Your Career.* Englewood Cliffs, N.J.: Prentice-Hall, 1978.

———— . *Educational Psychology.* Englewood Cliffs, N.J.: Prentice-Hall, 1979.

———— . "Constructive Peer Relationships, Social Development, and Cooperative Learning Experiences: Implications for the Prevention of Drug Abuse." *Journal of Drug Education* 10 (1980): 7-24.

———— . *Reaching Out: Interpersonal Effectiveness and Self-Actualization.* 2nd ed. Englewood Cliffs, N.J.: Prentice-Hall, 1981.

Johnson, D. W., and Johnson, R. *Joining Together: Group Theory and Group Skills.* Englewood Cliffs, N.J.: Prentice-Hall, 1982.

———— . *Learning Together and Alone: Cooperation, Competition, and Individualization.* Englewood Cliffs, N.J.: Prentice-Hall, 1975.

———— . "Cooperative, Competitive, and Individualistic Learning." *Journal of Research and Development in Education* 12 (1978): 3-15.

———— . "Conflict in the Classroom: Controversy and Learning." *Review of Educational Research* 49 (1979): 51-70.

———— . *The Effect of Effort and Interpersonal Attraction: Mainstreaming Hearing-Impaired Students.* University of Minnesota, submitted for publication, 1982.

———— . "The Socialization and Achievement Crisis: Are Cooperative Learning Experiences the Solution?" In *Applied Social Psychology Annual 4.* Edited by L. Bickman. Beverly Hills, Calif.: Sage Publications, 1983.

Johnson, D. W.; Johnson, R.; and Maruyama, G. "Interdependence and Interpersonal Attraction Among Heterogeneous and Homogeneous Individuals: A Theoretical Formulation and a Meta-Analysis of the Research." *Review of Educational Research* 53 (1983): 5-54.

Johnson, D. W.; Maruyama, G.; Johnson, R.; Nelson, D.; and Skon, L. "Effects of Cooperative, Competitive and Individualistic Goal Structures on Achievement: A Meta-Analysis." *Psychological Bulletin* 89 (1981): 47-62.

Johnson, R., and Johnson, D. W. "What Research Says About Student-Student Interaction in Science Classrooms." In *Education in the 80's: Science.* Edited by M. Rowe. Washington, D.C.: National Education Association, 1982, pp. 25-37.

Lawrence, G. *Patterns of Effective Inservice Education: A State of the Art Summary of Research on Materials and Procedures for Changing Teacher Behaviors in Inservice Education.* Tallahassee: Florida State Department of Education, 1974.

Lerner, B. "The Minimum Competence Testing Movement: Social, Scientific, and Legal Implications." *American Psychologist* 27 (1981): 1057-1066.

Little, J. *School success and staff development in urban desegregated schools.* Paper presented at the American Educational Research Association Convention, Los Angeles, April, 1981.

Lyons, V. (Ed.) *Structuring cooperative learning experiences in the classroom: The 1980 handbook.* Edina, Minn.: Interaction Book Company, 1980.

McLaughlin, M., & Marsh, D. Staff development and school change. *Teachers College Record,* 1978, *80,* 69-94.

Naisbitt, J. *Megatrends.* New York, N.Y.: Warner Books, 1982.

Roy, P (Ed.) *Structuring cooperative learning experiences in the classroom: The 1982 handbook.* Edina, Minn.: Interaction Book Company, 1982.

Schultz, T. *Investing in people.* Berkeley: University of California Press, 1981.

Science Education Data Book. Washington, D.C.: National Science Foundation, 1980.

Slavin, R. *The effects of teams in Teams-Games-Tournament on the normative climates of classrooms.* Baltimore: Center for Social Organization of Schools, Johns Hopkins University, 1974.

Walberg, H. *Education and scientific literacy.* University of Illinois, mimeographed report, 1982.

Wheeler, R., & Ryan, F. Effects of cooperative and competitive environments on the attitudes and achievement of elementary school students engaged in social studies inquiry activities. *Journal of Educational Psychology,* 1973, *65,* 402-407.

Wirszup, I. The Soviet challenge. *Educational Leadership,* 1981, *38,* 358-366.

Index